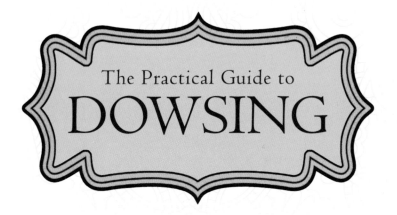

The Practical Guide to

DOWSING

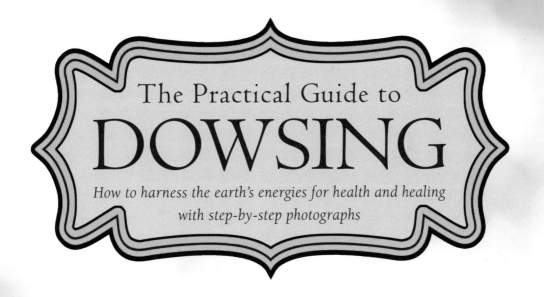

The Practical Guide to
DOWSING

*How to harness the earth's energies for health and healing
with step-by-step photographs*

Dr PATRICK MacMANAWAY

LORENZ BOOKS

This book is dedicated with love and admiration to my parents, Bruce and Patricia MacManaway, whose vision and integrity served the unqualified return of the spirit of healing and dowsing to the community.

Published by Lorenz Books
an imprint of Anness Publishing Limited
www.lorenzbooks.com
info@anness.com

A CIP catalogue record is available from the British Library

Publisher: Joanna Lorenz
Editorial Director: Helen Sudell
Designer: Nigel Partridge
Special photography: Don Last
Additional photographs: Shutterstock
Production Controller: Ben Worley

Note: The reader should not regard the recommendations, ideas and techniques expressed and described in this book as substitutes for the advice of a qualified medical practitioner. Any use to which the ideas and techniques are put is at the reader's sole discretion and risk.

Author's acknowledgments: My grateful thanks to Rosanagh Bennet, Ann Preston, Dr Duncan Johnson and Dr Andrew Morrice for their expert advice and assistance in the areas of aromatherapy, reflexology, allergies, nutrition and flower remedies, and to acknowledge the contribution of the late Professor Cedric Wilson to the field of holistic research into allergies. Thanks to Sig Lonegren for holding the flame and to my wife, Heather, for tending the fire.

The publishers would like to thank the Chalice Well Trust in Glastonbury for their kind permission to allow photography in the Chalice Well Gardens.

Contents

Introduction

The ability to dowse is a simple and natural gift of the human spirit, present in each one of us from birth. It is a method for bringing our awake, alert, rational consciousness into direct communication and dialogue with our intuition and inner wisdom.

When exploring and interpreting the world around us, we depend to a great extent on our five 'primary' senses – touch, taste, smell, hearing and sight. It is an often-mentioned paradox that while we are so dependent on their information, the nature of the respective sensory organs is to limit and filter to a manageable amount what would otherwise be an overwhelming quantity of sensory stimulation. For example, the eyes respond only to the range of electromagnetic frequencies that for us is the 'visual spectrum' – the rainbow palette that colours and defines the world and all that is in it. Yet this visual spectrum is but a wafer-thin band of a vast range of frequencies reaching far above and below the ability of our human senses to perceive them.

Intuition is sometimes described as the 'sixth sense', and although it remains the least understood it is perhaps the most powerful and primary sense of all. One of the central mysteries of life is the interconnectedness of all things. Through our intuition, we are able to perceive and experience this interconnectedness, and gather virtually unlimited information far beyond the reach of the other senses. The imagination is the sensory organ of the intuition, and while the rich textures of the imagination can guide and inspire us in a general way, to interpret intuitive information in a specific and detailed fashion requires focus and discipline.

Dowsing is just such a disciplined focus, bridging the gap between rational and intuitive, and giving us potentially unlimited access to information about the world of which we are an integral part. Using dowsing to explore and enhance our health is one of the most practical and affirming uses of this simple and natural miracle of human consciousness.

Doorway to Wholeness

The breeze at dawn has secrets to tell you.
Don't go back to sleep.
You must ask for what you really want.
Don't go back to sleep.
People are going back and forth across the doorsill
where the two worlds touch.
The door is round and open.
Don't go back to sleep.
RUMI (1207–1273)

Health and wholeness

This book is an invitation to explore a uniquely personal and radically powerful path to extraordinary health. It will guide you in opening and cultivating a dialogue with your inner self – or wisdom self. This part of you knows what your body needs to be healthy, knows what your mind needs for stimulation and satisfaction, and knows what your spirit needs.

The nature of health

What is health, and what does it mean to be healthy? We may often think and talk about health, both our own and that of other people, but what do we really mean by the term? Often when we talk about health we are referring to how well our body is functioning for us, and think of health in physical terms. People also speak about their health in feeling terms, and we may ask someone how they are feeling as a way of inquiring after their health. We might hear 'I'm feeling fine' or 'I'm not feeling very good today', and understand that our emotional state also plays a part in our concept of health.

We use the word 'health' in many different ways and to communicate somewhat different things, depending on the context and circumstances.

The World Health Organization defines it like this: 'Health is a state of complete physical, mental, and social well-being and not merely the absence of disease or infirmity.' This is a very helpful definition. It guides us to assess health in positive terms of well-being rather than in terms of impairment, and to include in our health assessment the nature and quality of our relationships, including our role as members of a community.

The word 'health' comes from the same root as the word 'whole'. Assessing health in terms of how far or fast we can run, how attractive we think we are, or how often or seldom we experience physical or emotional discomfort, leads us to a very limited sense of ourselves and our lives. Turning our attention towards how whole our lives can be and how complete and integrated we can become as human beings, both in relation to ourselves and to our

▲ The wise self knows who we are and what we need and will bring us towards experiences of joy and peace. This can be seen as the balanced interaction between body, mind and spirit.

community, leads us in an altogether more powerful, liberating, and genuinely interesting direction.

Seen in this context, health is perhaps not definable as an externally measured state but as a life fully experienced and lived.

The holistic paradigm

Increasingly, many of us are learning to assess health not only in terms of our minds and our bodies, but also to include the element of spirit.

'Spirit', rather like 'health', is a word that we all define a little differently, and this in itself tells us something important – that spirit is something whose nature is unique and quite individual. We would probably agree that it has to do with the deepest and truest part of ourselves, our essence or 'inner self'; related to, but different from, our physical body and our thoughts.

The holistic paradigm is one in which every part of a human being – body, mind and spirit – is considered. Furthermore, it is understood that these three elements are interwoven, interdependent, and reflective of each other.

In terms of health, this means that any physical imbalance is also associated with a related disturbance in the mind and spirit, and that for complete physical healing to occur, balance must be restored in all three dimensions of our being.

Discussing spirit in the context of health can make some of us feel uncomfortable. An acceptance of the reality of spirit and its relationship with the mind and body is as old at least as oral history, and has been forgotten only relatively recently as we have become increasingly fascinated by the development of science and new material technology. For many of us, matters of the spirit seem abstract and removed from our lives, and following a spiritual path seems incompatible with the pressures of modern life. However, by allowing our fears and concerns to dominate us, we may be missing an important point and one that could be highly rewarding and enriching.

Let us consider a paradox: it could be that we are not so much human beings who may choose to walk a spiritual path, but rather spiritual beings who have chosen to walk a human path. If this proposition is true, then it can change how we live our lives and our attitude to the world. From this perspective, health may be seen as the acceptance and expression of our uniqueness, allowing our true self to be totally present and fully engaged and allowing us to experience our lives as fully as we would wish.

Part of the process of reaching a state of greater self-acceptance and self-expression is trusting the inner self, and to receive its wisdom. This spirit self has a voice and one of the ways we can begin to listen closely to it is by learning how to dowse.

▼ Allowing space and time in our lives to listen to the small, still voice within, in whatever way feels most natural and comfortable, begins the process of aligning our physical and spiritual selves.

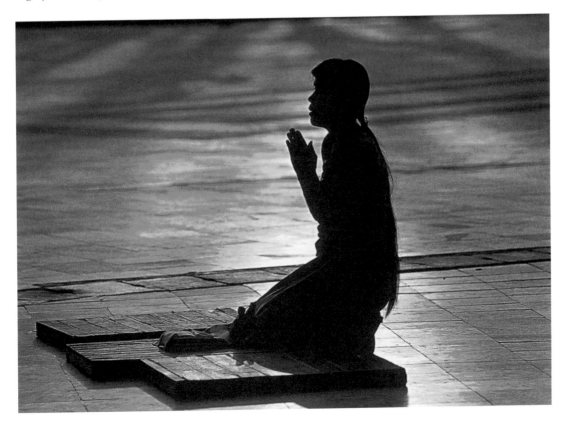

A doorway to the inner world

Dowsing is a simple and natural process, and is a universal human ability. It bridges the rational, intellectual part of ourselves with the intuitive part. Both an art and a science, dowsing is a holistic discipline, teaching us to develop and use our intellect and intuition together, and to engage in matters of concern with a sincere but unattached focus. The more respect that we bring to our dowsing, the more reliable it will be.

Studies monitoring the brainwaves that are generated by dowsers reveal a range of frequencies and a balance between the left and right hemispheres of the brain which is comparable with those of long-term meditators and yogis. This is indicative of both a balanced and an expanded sensory perception that is accessed through dowsing, to gently align body, mind and spirit.

Basic principles of dowsing

Dowsing works very simply. We ask a clear and unambiguous question in our mind, to which the answer can only be 'Yes' or 'No'. Having asked the

▼ The uses of dowsing are limited only by our imagination. This woodcut shows the use of dowsing to locate and extract mineral ore, a practice that continues to the present day.

Dowsing is a gateway to intuition, bridging the gap between the mind and spirit.

question, we allow the answer to come back to us from our inner self, using a predetermined code to interpret the movements of the dowsing tool in order to indicate whether it is a positive or a negative response. The process of dowsing is used to discover information that we either cannot get in any other way or that we do not have quick or easy access to. A genuine need to know the answer is key for dowsing to work well, along with 'unattached curiosity'. This means having a calm and open mind as to what the answer will be. If we are too emotionally attached to a particular outcome, this can negatively influence our dowsing.

When we pose a dowsing question, we are asking with the rational, intellectual, thinking part of our mind. Then, having asked the question, we wait, patiently and with engaged but unattached curiosity, for the answer to come back to us. There is little we can do to influence the outcome, except to ask the most salient question. The answer comes back to us almost immediately, in the form of a symbolic movement. This is the voice of our intuition, using our dowsing tool as a mouthpiece.

Intellect and intuition

To dowse well, we must ask the right questions, and in doing so we learn to focus our mind on asking questions that are appropriate and timely. When we are dowsing, we need to remain alert and aware of ourselves, exercising reason and discrimination. It is not about completely surrendering ourselves to intuition and irrational forces. This means that dowsing can be integrated into every part of our lives without disruption or disturbance and help us towards an experience of increasing wholeness.

DOWSING TOOLS

The most familiar tools that dowsers use nowadays are the pendulum, the L-rod, the Y-rod or forked stick, the bobber and, more recently, the aurameter. The movement of the dowsing tool or instrument is caused by the movement of the dowser's muscles. However, for the dowser the experience is that the tool is moving by itself. This is because the action is not voluntary or intended but occurs involuntarily, in the same way as a yawn, a laugh, a heartbeat or a breath. The dowsing movement occurs completely naturally without our needing to make it happen.

▶ The simple pendulum is universally popular, versatile and convenient. It can be anything from a ring or a crystal weight on a thread. Although often very personalized, anything that swings freely will serve as an effective pendulum. Many pendulums are made from wood, others from polished stones or crystals, sometimes plastics, and many from metals of various kinds. The choice is really up to you.

▲ L-rods are excellent field-tools, and are particularly useful for searching and locating in dowsing tasks. They can be quickly and inexpensively made by bending any piece of wire to form a right-angle, with the arm longer than the handle.

▲ The bobber or wand is a traditional dowsing tool, and can be made by cutting a springy branch and holding its narrow end, so that it can easily bounce or bob. Metal bobbers can also be bought and used in the same way and are just as effective.

▲ The Y-rod or V-rod is a time-honoured and still popular dowsing tool, much favoured by water and mineral dowsers. Traditionally it is cut from a tree, often hazel, willow or apple, but modern plastics also work just as well.

▲ Many custom-made and sophisticated dowsing tools are also available. This aurameter combines high-tensile wire with a spring-swivel in the handle to create a delightfully sensitive and highly visual dowsing tool.

The journey begins

When learning to dowse, a pendulum is an excellent tool for the beginner, and for many remains forever their tool of choice. The pendulum is perhaps the most convenient as well as the most versatile of dowsing tools.

Choosing a pendulum

To make a pendulum suitable for dowsing, we need something that can be suspended from a thread, chain, piece of string or other cord. Ideally a pendulum is symmetrical and attached to its cord centrally, so that it can swing perfectly freely in any direction. If this does not happen, and it has any tendency to an asymmetrical or unbalanced motion, this can compromise its use in dowsing.

Almost anything that swings freely and easily can be used as a pendulum. This can include a ring suspended on a piece of thread, a hexagonal nut tied to a piece of string, or even keys on a chain. After a while, most dowsers find a pendulum that 'feels right' and which they use consistently when dowsing. Much like an artist's favourite paintbrush or maybe a carpenter's best tool, dowsers tend to develop a familiarity and ease with a particular weight and balance in their hand, and often develop a preference for a pendulum made from a particular material. Don't get too attached to your pendulum, however, remember that dowsing is an inner process, and that your pendulum is a tool for discovering wisdom and not the source of it.

Creating your own signals

If you find that your dowsing responses are not working or don't come easily, don't worry. Many of us have a bit of difficulty in getting dowsing to work when we first start. We are trying to establish a connection with a part of ourselves that may have been dormant for quite a long time, so we can afford to be patient and take the time to wake it up slowly and gently.

DOWSING PREPARATION
Although it's not strictly necessary to sit or stand in a special way, a good posture helps to relax the body and keep the mind alert. Either sit or stand with your feet firmly and evenly balanced on the floor, about shoulder-width apart, and hold your spine erect.

1 Hold the cord of your pendulum between the thumb and forefinger of your dominant hand (that means the right hand for right-handed people and the left hand for left-handed people) with the tips of the thumb and forefinger pointing downwards to allow the pendulum to swing freely. The greater the distance between your fingers and the pendulum, the longer

and slower the pendulum will move. In contrast, if you hold the pendulum on a very short cord, it will swing about in a quick, lively fashion. There is no right or wrong length, but a distance of 5–8 cm (2–3 in) generally gives a nice responsive action.

2 Hold your pendulum centrally between and a little above the height of your knees and start it swinging in a to-and-fro motion towards and away from you. This is the neutral or search position, and means 'I am ready to start dowsing'.

BASIC DOWSING RESPONSES

What we need to establish next are the pendulum motions that will mean 'Yes' and 'No' for you. These vary from person to person and the key is knowing what your personal dowsing responses are.

1 With your pendulum swinging back and forth, move your hand over until your pendulum is swinging over your dominant-side knee (right side for right-handers, left side for left-handers) and state clearly and simply in your mind 'Please show me my 'Yes' response'.

2 Pay close attention to what the pendulum does. It may change its back and forth swing to a clockwise or anti-clockwise motion, it may alter the direction of its swing from towards and away from you to a diagonal swing or even a side-to-side swing, or it might stop swinging altogether. Whatever it does, this will now be your signal for 'Yes'.

3 Now take your pendulum back to its neutral swing between your knees, and this time move your hand over until your pendulum is swinging over your non-dominant side knee and state clearly and simply in your mind 'Please show me my 'No' response'.

4 Closely observe what your pendulum does – it should change its swing to something clearly different from either your 'Neutral' or 'Yes' response. This new response is your signal for 'No'.

5 Repeat the exercise several times to become confident and familiar with your responses, taking your pendulum between the 'Neutral', 'Yes' and 'No' positions and allowing the responses to develop fully over each knee.

PENDULUM RESPONSES

The diagrams on the right show classic pendulum dowsing responses. You will see the introductory neutral which is a 'towards and away from you' swing, and the 'clockwise for Yes' and 'anti-clockwise for No' responses. While by no means universal, many dowsers find that these or a version of these, are the responses that their pendulum gives them when dowsing. Dowsing responses are a very individual and personal thing however, and you need not worry if yours are different; it only matters that they feel natural and right for you, and that you know which is which.

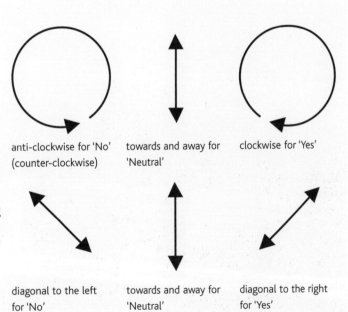

anti-clockwise for 'No' (counter-clockwise)

towards and away for 'Neutral'

clockwise for 'Yes'

diagonal to the left for 'No'

towards and away for 'Neutral'

diagonal to the right for 'Yes'

Dowsing exercises

Having established our pendulum's signals for 'Yes' and 'No', we have opened the doorway for a dialogue that can allow us to follow many paths and to apply dowsing usefully in our and even other peoples lives. To begin with however, some fun but simple exercises will allow us to practise crossing backwards and forwards between our rational intellect and intuition, getting swift, clear dowsing responses and learning to keep an open mind, in a state of engaged non-attachment.

Cup and ball exercise

Ideally, practice exercises in dowsing should be fun and engaging. They should involve our asking questions to which the answer can only be 'Yes' or 'No'; any ambiguity will make this exercise very difficult. Also, we should be able to get instant feedback on whether our dowsing was correct or not. Simple hiding games such as hiding a ball under a cup and dowsing to find its position, are easy to set up.

Playing cards exercise

A slightly more complex and longer exercise can be done with playing cards. Take an ordinary pack of playing cards and remove the jokers. Lie the pack face-down in front of you. We will begin by identifying whether the top card belongs to one of the black suits (clubs and spades) or to one of the red suits (diamonds and hearts).

Sitting comfortably, with your spine erect and your body relaxed, focus on the card at the top of the pile. You may wish to rest a finger on it to help you focus more completely, or even take it off the pack and place it face down on the table on its own. Start your pendulum in its to-and-fro, neutral swing, and ask clearly in your mind: 'Does this card belong to one of the black suits?'

Hold the question in your mind without worrying whether the card is black or red, and observe as your pendulum changes its motion from the to-and-fro of the neutral swing to either your 'Yes' or 'No' response. Once you have your response – in this case a 'Yes' would indicate a black card and a 'No' would indicate a red card – turn the card over and see whether your dowsing was correct. It was? Congratulations! It wasn't? Not to worry, try again.

Work your way gradually through the whole pack. As you do so, allow your mind to become

▼ Set up practice exercises so that a full answer is either yes or no, and where feedback is instant.

▼ The innocent nature of hide and seek games is ideal for engaging both intellect and intuition.

▲ Some exercises appeal more than others, and it will be easiest to get good dowsing responses from an exercise that captures your curiosity and attention. You could try a similar but simplified version of number dowsing using a set of dominoes.

increasingly patient and relaxed: stay alert, but let go of all attachment to which colour the card will be or even to whether or not your dowsing is accurate. Paradoxically, greater accuracy comes as we let go of our need to control the outcome and of our investment in being right or wrong.

As you go through the pack, put the cards that you dowsed correctly into one pile and the cards that you dowsed incorrectly into another. This will allow you to monitor your progress.

You will probably find that the state of open-minded, engaged non-attachment is easiest to achieve when you are alone, at least to begin with, and that consistent accuracy becomes harder in the presence of onlookers who you wish to convince or impress. Don't stake your reputation on your dowsing this early in your career! However, it can be fun and encouraging to share our exploration of dowsing with friends. It is also very helpful to practice with skilled and experienced dowsers.

Refining your skill

If you enjoyed the card-dowsing exercise, you can take it a step further, and dowse each card to find out exactly which member of the pack it is. In order to do this, we have to stay with questions to which the whole and complete answer is an unambiguous 'Yes' or 'No'. By asking carefully, we can narrow the possibilities down by half each time.

Start by asking if the card is black. Let's assume the answer is 'Yes'. Next ask if it is a member of the suit of clubs – let's say the answer now is a 'No'. With only two questions, we have found that the card is a member of the suit of spades. But which one is it?

A good question will reduce our options by half. 'Is this card higher than a seven?' (You need to decide whether you are counting aces high or low). Let's assume the answer is 'Yes' this time. Divide the possibilities in half again: 'Is this a court-card?' We get the answer 'No'. At this point, we have only three options: it is either the eight, nine or ten of spades. Once you have narrowed the possibilities down this far, it is easy to simply ask which number it is, one by one: 'Is this card the eight of spades?' 'No'. 'Is this card the nine of spades?' 'Yes.' Now turn the card over.

You may find that this is an easy exercise and that you get consistently accurate answers. If not, please don't be discouraged. Some of the very best dowsers have had to be patient in the beginning to cultivate consistently accurate responses.

▼ The great number of possibilities offered by a pack of cards helps us to learn to keep dowsing question-asking clear, efficient and unambiguous.

Talking more with your pendulum

Now that we have gained some basic skill with our pendulum, we can develop our dowsing vocabulary a little further to prepare us for working in real-life situations.

For the beginner, the response from the pendulum is the most mysterious and unfamiliar part of dowsing. After a little practice however, the movements of the pendulum or other dowsing tool become perfectly automatic and natural, and then the main task of dowsing becomes one of asking clear, concise, and unambiguous questions.

Ideally, a dowsing question should always be framed in such a way that either 'Yes' or 'No' is a complete and accurate response. Sometimes this

> **Let your imagination roam free and the realms of your knowledge will stretch towards infinity.**

is hard to do – particularly when we are dowsing about topic areas where we are relatively ignorant. If dowsing to identify a mechanical problem in our car, for example, those of us with expert mechanical knowledge will be able to ask specific, focused and relevant questions. Others may have a little knowledge, and ask questions that they think are precise, but which in fact are ambiguous and could be misleading if answered, 'Yes' or 'No'.

Recognizing the limits of intellectual knowledge and understanding is important and even humbling at times. It is often best to start our inquiry from absolute basics, with a beginner's mind, thereby minimizing the pitfalls of our assumptions.

Dowsing responses

In addition to asking careful questions, however, we can also get a helpful guiding nudge from our intuition to steer us back on track when we start to stray. This is made possible by three additional dowsing responses: 'Yes, but…', 'No, but…' and 'Unanswerable question'. The former two signals are of immense help in guiding us to ask more complete and precise questions, and can save us from getting hopelessly misled, while the latter can be particularly helpful when we are pursuing a misleading path. When you get one of these responses, it alerts you to the fact that your question cannot be completely or accurately answered, or that you are going in the wrong direction.

As before, sit comfortably and relaxed with your spine erect and your feet shoulder-width apart on the floor. Hold your pendulum in the search position and establish your to-and-fro neutral swing. Move your pendulum over your dominant-side knee and let it develop into its full 'Yes' signal.

OTHER BASIC PENDULUM RESPONSES
Very often if a 'Yes' is a fully developed circular motion, either clockwise or anti-clockwise, the 'Yes, but…' will be an ellipse in the same direction, the degree of certainty being expressed by the fullness of the circle that develops. Similarly if your 'Yes' signal is a diagonal swing, for example half-left to half-right, the 'Yes, but…' may be an incompletely developed diagonal, say quarter-left to quarter-right. 'No' responses would then be the opposite. 'Unanswerable question' is typically marked by a side-to-side swing.

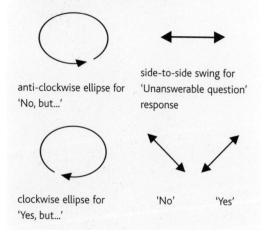

anti-clockwise ellipse for 'No, but…'

side-to-side swing for 'Unanswerable question' response

clockwise ellipse for 'Yes, but…'

'No'   'Yes'

Now, bring it back one-third of the way towards the midline, neutral position, and as you do so, ask clearly in your mind to be shown your Yes, but...' signal. This may be a half-developed 'Yes' signal – which may be an almost lazy 'sort of yes' answer, or it may be a new direction of swing from any of your previous responses.

Bring your pendulum back to your midline neutral position and swing, and then go over your non-dominant knee and let it develop its normal 'No' response. Now bring it back one-third of the way towards the midline and ask clearly in your mind to be shown your 'No, but...' signal.

Finally, go back to your neutral swing, and ask clearly in your mind to be now shown your 'Unanswerable question' response. Often this response is a side-to-side swing, although it may be anything provided it is clear and different from your other responses. You do not need to move the pendulum – this signal will develop in the midline.

As with your original establishment of the 'Yes' and 'No' signals, if your pendulum does not

▼ To use a dowsing chart, hold the pendulum over the base of the chart and start with your neutral swing on the centre line. Ask your question and allow the pendulum to point towards a response.

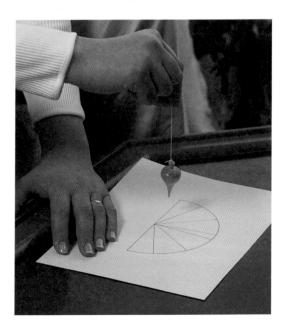

RESPONSE EXERCISE CHART

Now you have learned all of the responses you will need to begin working with your pendulum. You can practise them using an enlarged version of the dowsing chart shown below to help you. Simply hold your pendulum above each section and the pendulum response should correspond with the movements you have just worked out.

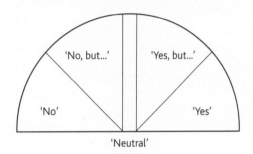

spontaneously offer you these three signals, you can choose yourself what they will be and swing the pendulum in the 'Yes, but...', 'No, but...' and 'Unanswerable question' motions of your choice while affirming: 'This is my signal for 'Yes, but...'' and so forth. You can do this in conjunction with the dowsing response chart.

Whether they come to you spontaneously or by your active choice, repeatedly practise the different responses in their appropriate positions until they feel automatic and entirely natural.

Response reversal

Sometimes, when we are tired, or under considerable stress, or if we are dowsing for something which is close to us emotionally, our dowsing responses may become reversed, so that our normal 'Yes' becomes our 'No' and our normal 'No' becomes our 'Yes'. This does not seem to affect all dowsers equally. Some dowsers never experience this phenomenon at all. Others experience it intermittently, particularly when they are first learning The wisest strategy is to check your 'Yes/No' signal each time you begin to dowse. Then you can be sure that you and your pendulum are speaking the same language.

It's all in the state of the mind

Once we have become clear about our responses and familiar with the use of the pendulum, we can start to use dowsing on a regular basis in our everyday life. Through much of this book we will be learning ways to use dowsing for enhancing our health and well-being. Part of integrating dowsing into our lives is to allow it to be a straightforward and matter-of-fact activity. It can be helpful to approach your dowsing as though you were asking the advice of someone you love and respect.

The dowsing sequence

There is a sequence which we follow when dowsing. It has a beginning, a middle and an end.

We begin by clearing our mind of clutter, busyness and preconceptions, and centering ourselves in an alert but peaceful way in our body. How this is done is very individual, and you will discover what works best for you. Avoid dowsing when you are tired or upset as it is difficult to be clear and focused during these times.

Sit or stand quietly for a minute or two and start to become aware of your breathing. Visualize yourself in a column of golden light, radiating to you from the Divine, the source of universal love. This will enhance and balance the body-mind-spirit connection.

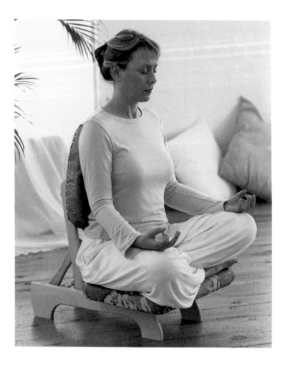

▲ Find a way that feels natural to clear your mind and centre yourself peacefully in your body before you start to dowse. An alert and engaged, but unattached, state of mind helps us to do our best dowsing. Meditative breathing is one preparation.

ENGAGED NON-ATTACHMENT

While we are dowsing, aim for a state of engaged non-attachment. This becomes easier to attain the more we become familiar with the state. It is important, because we can otherwise influence the result of our dowsing by our mind wishing that the response will be either 'Yes' or 'No'. When we are first learning to dowse (or even when we are experienced) two things can be helpful in engaging the mind so that it does not distort or influence the outcome: continuing to repeat the question that we have asked until our dowsing response is fully established, and retaining a child-like curiosity and wonder in the outcome.

TIMELY AND APPROPRIATE

Sometimes your dowsing may tell you 'No' when you ask if your questions are timely and appropriate. There are cycles of time which unfold at their own speed, and sometimes answers are not available until their unfolding is complete. Also, there is some information that it may not be appropriate for us to know. Sometimes we have to wait for further pieces of the jigsaw of our life or someone else's life to have been put into place, revealing the emerging pattern of wholeness. A healthy respect for what is timely and appropriate and a philosophical acceptance of 'what is' is part of being a good dowser.

You can offer a prayer or ask for help and guidance from a particular spiritual source. Stay with what feels right to you, and be sure that you are centred in your heart. Once you are clear, centred and connected, dowsing can begin. Sitting or standing comfortably and relaxed, set your pendulum into its neutral swing, over your dominant knee as before, and check your 'Yes' response.

Next, state clearly in your mind the topic you wish to dowse about, to 'tune in'. Now ask: 'Is it timely and appropriate for me to dowse about this?' If your dowsing tells you 'No', then give thanks to your spirit for guiding you, and leave the topic for another time. If 'Yes', then you can proceed.

You may now ask as many questions as you need to discover all the information that can help. Try to ask questions that will be answered by 'Yes' or 'No', and pay attention and rethink if you get 'Yes, but...', 'No, but...' or 'Unanswerable question'.

When you think you are finished it is wise to ask: 'Is there anything else that I need to know about this now?' It is also a good idea to make sure that you aren't ending with any misconceptions. State clearly in your mind the key information and conclusions, and then ask: 'Is this the truth?' Finally, give thanks for the guidance received.

▼ Dowsing blind helps us to ask questions that we are emotionally attached to without compromising our dowsing.

DOWSING SEQUENCE SUMMARY

Clear, centre and connect

Start neutral swing and check 'Yes'

State dowsing topic

Ask: 'Is this timely and appropriate?'

Dowse all necessary questions

Ask: 'Do I need any more information about this now?'

State conclusion

Ask: 'Is this the truth?'

Give thanks for help and guidance

Blind dowsing

Sometimes, you might encounter a situation where dowsing would be of benefit but where you are so involved that you cannot be sure that your hopes or fears will not influence the outcome. One technique to use at such a time is to dowse 'blind'. This means that you dowse without knowing what question you are asking.

Write your questions on the subject down on separate but identical pieces of paper. As well as the questions which you want to dowse, you can also write some simple, factual 'control' questions to which you already know the answer, such as 'Is today Tuesday? Is my name...?' These will help you to check the accuracy of your dowsing, which may be compromised if you are tired or upset. Turn the pieces of paper face-down and shuffle them.

Dowse over the papers one by one asking: 'What is the answer to the question on this piece of paper?' Make a pile of 'Yes' responses and another pile of 'No' responses. Once you have dowsed them all, turn the papers over. The accuracy of your dowsing over the control questions will guide you in interpreting the answers to your concerns.

If your dowsing is inaccurate, you might ask someone less involved to dowse for you (if it is important, you can also have them dowse blind to check their own accuracy).

Pathway to Health

Truth is within ourselves, it takes no rise
From outward things, whate'er you may believe
There is an inner centre in us all
Where truth abides in fullness; and around
Wall upon wall the gross flesh hems it in
That perfect clear perception which is Truth.
A baffling and perverting carnal mesh
Binds all and makes all error, but to know
Rather consists in finding out a way
For the imprisoned splendour to escape
Than in achieving entry for a light
Supposed to be without.
ROBERT BROWNING (1812–1889)

Finding true health

Dowsing for information and guidance around our health is one of its most valuable uses, and also one of the best ways to build up dowsing experience and confidence. It is an area of dowsing in which the need is genuine and life-affirming, and where the feedback is direct and personally experienced.

Whether dowsing to help us recover from an illness or to enhance our overall well-being, the process of bringing focused attention to our health and of integrating our thoughts and activities with the new information and wisdom from our spirit brings into play a powerful alignment of psychic, mental and physical energies. A spiritual law says that whatever we give our energy or attention to is both magnified and attracted to us. Therefore by actively seeking health, we attract it to us in every area of our lives.

Empowerment basics

Our lives are so diverse and complex and so many of our decisions are made 'on the run' that we can quickly feel overwhelmed by the thought of taking time to dowse for basic decision making. So start slowly, and with one area of your life at a time. The following pages offer focused discussion and practical guidance on a number of strategies for enhancing health that you can explore using dowsing. As you read through them, take the time to dowse for yourself and explore how these different topics might have relevance in your life. You will surely find the time wisely invested. Far from being an additional, burdensome step in decision

▼ Dowsing helps us resource our inner ability to deal with life's challenges, and our enhanced well-being offers its own rich rewards.

making, you will find that the new information discovered through dowsing leads to simple but profound changes in patterns of thought and behaviour, and that even a small investment of dowsing time can send far-reaching ripples into your life. If you like the changes that occur as a result of your dowsing, you will soon find your pendulum to be a close friend and constant companion. The more that you practise your dowsing, the easier you will find it to frame useful and relevant questions, and the quicker you will find your answers.

One of the biggest and most fundamental shifts in awareness that occurs for many people when they start to experience their lives enhanced by dowsing, is the deep-seated knowledge and understanding that we really do know, deep down and for ourselves, what healthy looks and feels like and that we really can take the initiative and power to claim that for ourselves. Freedom, self-empowerment, and personal responsibility are the natural consequences of this experience.

Healthy reactions

Moving towards a state of health that is natural, for most of us, involves letting go of long-established, unhealthy thoughts and behaviour patterns, of limiting and fear-based emotions, and of physical toxins of various kinds that our body has accumulated and stored, unable to rid itself of them. As we do this, we may well experience a cleansing process as the old, blocked energy and physical toxins are mobilized and released for excretion.

This can make us feel physically unwell and emotionally upset. This is a natural part of a constructive healing process and of the return to health, and when it occurs in an intense fashion it is often termed a healing crisis. This is not something to be feared, but is to be welcomed and embraced. We can see it as a threshold over which we need to pass in order to find a new, more healthy place for ourselves and our lives.

Many of the healing strategies and some of the techniques described in this book may precipitate such a cleansing, detoxifying, healing crisis either in yourself, or in others who you are helping to heal. It may last for a few seconds or minutes, or it

▲ As you move through this cleansing period, balance will gradually be restored and a great sense of vitality and peace will be experienced.

may last for hours or sometimes for days. An initial cleansing period of three days is very commonly experienced. Try to ride through it with a gently positive and hopeful attitude, as you will surely feel better for it and feel revitalized when it is over.

Supporting the healing force

To move through this period, it is helpful for us to be optimally supported in body, mind and spirit. The body can be helped by an intake of plenty of water, and a simple cleansing diet of bland, mostly raw whole foods, fresh fruit and root vegetables. Cook by steaming or boiling rather than frying. For the mind and spirit, allow yourself as much rest as possible apart from gentle outdoor exercise, and avoid becoming overly tired. Spend time engaged in activities that you enjoy. Allow yourself periods of quiet contemplation and meditation, and picture yourself becoming entirely whole and completely healthy.

The food that we eat

'We are what we eat' is a well-worn phrase, but a true one nevertheless. Our physical body is a truly awe-inspiring miracle. Constantly building, repairing, adapting and regulating itself, balancing a myriad chemical reactions and complex biological processes, it has a level of organization and infrastructure comparable to a large city.

Our food provides the wide variety of raw materials as well as the fuel for all of this activity, and comprehensively serving our body's diverse nutritional needs is a key to keeping it functioning at its peak level of health and vitality.

Our body is remarkably tolerant of inadequate nutrition, but only for short periods; our long-term health is inextricably linked to our long-term diet. The experience of being optimally nourished – both by feeding our body all the things that it truly needs and by avoiding foods or other substances that are harmful or toxic to it – is radically different from the experience of simply getting by on a make-do diet based on convenience and circumstance.

▼ From dietary choice to assessing the ripeness of fruit, a pendulum is a useful tool in the kitchen.

DOWSING DIET ANALYSIS
Our intuitive self knows what our body needs for vibrant health. Make an dowsing analysis of your diet. Here are some pointers to start with:

• Identify any foods that are missing from your diet, any that are present in excess, and any that your body would rather not have.
• Increase your daily intake of water to 2 litres/3½ pints per day to improve hydration and to regulate appetite; water also assists toxin elimination which may occur as you begin to reform your diet.
• Start to compile a list of all the foods which your dowsing indicates you need.
• The process of tailoring your diet is necessarily slow – dowse once a week over a period of three months and keep adding to or amending your list. Keep a diary of the dietary and health changes that you experience.

Finding our optimum diet

There are many resources available to inform us and help us make healthy eating choices. Important considerations include the range, type and quality of food, as well as the balance of proteins, carbohydrates and fats. In addition, we need to ensure we have sufficient fibre, an adequate and balanced intake of vitamins and minerals, and plenty of fresh water. Whatever kind of food we eat, the best quality foodstuff is organic, grown in a mineral- rich, living soil, which has not been treated by pesticides or chemicals, and consumed as near fresh as possible.

Food preparation is important too, with choices between eating raw or cooked food, and if the latter, how it is cooked. This is an area of our lives where our inner wisdom combined with our dowsing can act as tremendously helpful tools and allies, guiding and supporting us in making the healthiest and most life-affirming decisions about the food we eat.

▲ Generally speaking, food that is raw, fresh and organic has more to offer a healthy diet than over-cooked and processed foods.

Dowsing our diet

Take some time to sit quietly and reflect on your diet. What did you eat today? Yesterday? Make a list of everything that you have eaten in the last three days and you may have some surprises – what we actually eat and what we think we eat can be two quite different things.

Take out your pendulum, centre yourself and clear your mind. Let yourself come to a place of non-attachment – our relationship with food can be very tied up with meeting emotional, rather than nutritional needs. Check your 'Yes' response. 'Is it timely and appropriate for me to dowse about my diet?' If 'Yes' proceed with questions that are answered by 'Yes' or 'No'.

'Does my present diet meet all of my protein needs? Do I need to add new sources of protein to my diet? Would my protein needs be best met by adding eggs to my diet? Would one egg per week be sufficient to meet my needs at this time? Should I add other sources of protein?'

You can use your pendulum to dowse directly over specific foods, checking to see if they are right for your body. You can also dowse as you prepare each meal. Although laborious at first, you will find that the process speeds up dramatically as you become familiar with your body's needs, and develop an increasingly intuitive feel for what your body might like.'Does this meal contain everything that my body needs right now? Do I need to add more fat and oil? A serving of sunflower seeds? Is there anything I should eliminate from this meal?'

DIETARY REQUIREMENTS

Dramatic improvements in mood, concentration, sleep quality, strength, endurance, disease resistance and overall vitality occur when all of our nutritional needs are met. Tailoring our diet to perfectly meet all of our body's needs is a wonderful gift that we can give to ourselves. Learning about food and nutrition is of immense and lasting value. Each one of us is different, however, and it is difficult, even for the well-informed, to fully assess the nutritional needs of a unique individual. Harder still is the challenge of assessing and adapting our diet to keep pace with the constant changes our body encounters at various points in life, such as growing up, pregnancy and breast feeding, changing work and leisure activity, and ageing, and the gradual variation in physical activity and food availability that follows the annual cycle of seasonal change.

Use these guidelines as a starting point for your optimum diet, compiled with the help of dowsing:
protein (c.15% of diet): eggs, pulses, soya, quinoa, cheese, meat and fish.
fats and oils (c.15% of diet): fresh fish, nut and seed oils.
carbohydrate (c.70% of diet): whole grains (rice, oats, whole wheat), green and root vegetables, and fresh fruit.
fibre: whole grains, nuts and seeds, vegetables and fruit.
minerals: whole grains, pulses, seeds, green and root vegetables.
vitamins: nuts and seeds, fresh and raw green and root vegetables and fresh fruit.
subtle energy: raw, fresh fruit and vegetables, especially green and root vegetables.
water: plenty of filtered, uncarbonated water.

Food vitality, vitamins and minerals

As well as its physical nutritional properties, food carries the 'life-force' or vital essence of the plant or animal that it comes from. This is most intensely present when the food is at its freshest, and gradually diminishes over time and through processing and cooking. Food that has high life-force seems to taste better and gives us more nourishment. Often we find we need to eat less of a food to feel satisfied if its vitality is strong. Food with high vitality adds a shine to our eyes and a bounce to our step.

Vitality chart

Dowse over your food to assess its vitality. Because vitality slowly diminishes, a scale is useful. The suggested scale is 1 to 10, with 0 indicating no life-force, and 10 meaning fully vital. You can use the chart shown here, or else choose your own scale and create your own chart. 'Is the vitality of this rice higher than 5? Higher than 8? Does it have a vitality of 10?'. You will almost surely find that fruit and vegetables just picked will have the highest 'score', and wholefoods will also be high on the vitality scale. In comparison, packaged foods with long shelf lives will have a lower score.

Vitamins and minerals

Proteins, fats and oils, and carbohydrates are the three main food groups, and we need an appropriate and balanced quantity of these on a daily basis to maintain and fuel our body. Equally important,

▲ Food vitality varies widely depending on growing and harvesting conditions, storage, packaging and processing. Although subtle and unseen, the vitality of food is a significant part of its nutritional value.

however, is our intake of vitamins and minerals. We need these in relatively small amounts, but their presence in our diet is essential. Minerals are an integral part of much of our body's structure, and both vitamins and minerals are required for many of the chemical and biological reactions and interactions that our body continually performs.

VITALITY CHART
To use the vitality chart, hold your pendulum behind the baseline of the chart, begin your neutral swing and ask to be shown the vitality of the food in question.

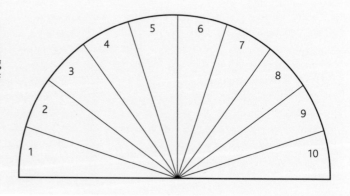

Many common health complaints stem from mineral or vitamin deficiencies, and supplementing our intake can have dramatic effects.

Ideally, we would obtain our necessary vitamin and mineral requirements by eating an appropriately diverse and balanced diet. Unfortunately, this can be difficult to achieve. Much of the food available to us today is grown in very depleted soils and is then treated and refined in ways which remove the minerals and vitamins from it.

Vitamin and mineral requirements are hard to assess other than by the presence or absence of deficiency or toxicity symptoms. Hair analysis is helpful for assessing long-term mineral status. Strands of hair can be sent off for special laboratory tests which indicate how much or how little of particular minerals there are in the body. Toxicity occurs if a vitamin or mineral is excessively present in our diet, as liquid or solid. Mineral toxicity sometimes occurs from drinking water. You can have your drinking water checked for this.

Dowsing for supplements

We can use dowsing as a way of letting our body tell us what it needs for optimum health. Centre and balance yourself and check your 'Yes' response. 'I want to assess my current vitamin and mineral needs. Is this timely and appropriate?'. If 'Yes' then you can proceed.

'Does my present diet meet all of my vitamin requirements? Would a multi-vitamin preparation be the best way for me to meet my vitamin requirements? Is there one brand which would best meet my current needs? Do I need other specific vitamin supplements in addition to a multi-vitamin preparation? Is there anything else I should take?'

You will find a broad range of vitamin and mineral supplements at health-food stores as well as in most pharmacies. Try and meet your needs from as few products as you can. You may want to take your pendulum to the store and dowse discreetly along the shelf to find the best combination of supplements, or you might take a note of what is available and dowse over the list at home.

Dowse for the most appropriate combination of vitamins and minerals for yourself – your dowsing may also indicate that one brand is more suita-

▲ When choosing supplements, dowsing helps us to select the products that are most suitable for our unique needs. Reassessing these from time to time will accommodate any changes in life or lifestyle.

ble for your needs than another brand. Frame all of your questions so that they can be answered fully with a 'Yes' or 'No', and before finishing your dowsing session, ask 'Is there anything else that I need to know about this now?'

Compile a list of the following minerals and dowse over it to find out what you need: calcium, chromium, copper, iron, magnesium, manganese, selenium, zinc, cobalt, iodine, molbdenum, phosphorous, potassium, silicon, sodium and sulphur.

Once you have chosen your supplements, read the labels carefully and calculate the total doses of each vitamin and mineral that you will be taking. Many nutritional experts feel that the Recommended Daily Amounts (RDAs) on labelling are too low, however some vitamins and minerals can be harmful taken in excess, so do not exceed the amounts suggested by the manufacturers, doctor, or other expert on nutrition. Fully meeting our vitamin and mineral needs has a huge impact on our health. The effect may be noticed within a few weeks, but it is particularly of benefit to our mid- to long-term health and may not be noticed for some time.

The trouble with allergies

Our immune system develops from infancy and is responsible for maintaining the integrity of our physical body. It distinguishes between things that are beneficial or harmful to us. Some things are neither one nor the other, and can simply be ignored. But when the immune system encounters something potentially harmful, it activates various mechanisms for neutralizing or eliminating the threat. Most of the time it does this quietly without our noticing. An exception to this quiet and efficient functioning is when our body mounts an allergic response. This occurs when the body over-reacts to something benign or minimally harmful as though it were toxic. We may react to things in our diet, the air that we breathe or something we touch at home or at work, and experience rashes, poor digestion, sinus irritation and more.

In essence, allergies are disorders in our relationsip with things around us, and are reflected in our thoughts and feelings – body, mind and spirit together. There are different degrees of allergic response, those which are very minor are known as sensitivities. These mostly go unnoticed, but both allergies and sensitivities deplete our vitality, keeping us from an experience of optimal health.

▼ Using the body-mind-spirit connection, we can help desensitize ourselves to allergens by holding the thought of the allergen and the desensitizing number, which can be represented on a chart, or just pictured in our mind.

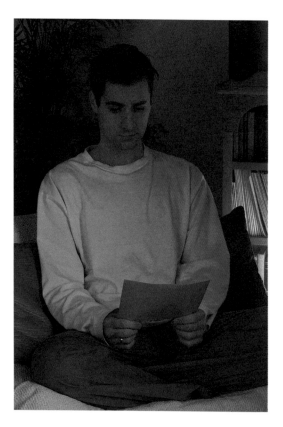

Detecting allergies

The technique here uses dowsing to detect allergies and sensitivities and desensitizes them using the power of the body-mind-spirit connection. It can bring tremendous relief to allergy sufferers and a significant increase in vitality. Note however, this technique is generally successful but cannot be guaranteed. For this reason, even after desensitization, those people with serious allergies should never expose themselves to allergens except under close medical supervision. Dowsing should not be used as an alternative or substitution for professional medical advice for severe allergies.

Things that we are allergic or sensitive to are called allergens. To identify allergens in your diet or environment, you can either dowse things as they occur to you, as you meet them, or, more efficiently, you can dowse lists of possible allergens.

Start by writing out a list of all the main items in your diet, and of all the things which you are in common contact with, at home and at work. This may take some time, but the rewards can be worth the trouble. Use the list of common allergens shown above to help you and add any that you already suspect may cause you trouble.

The more specific you can be, the better. If you find that you have a pollen allergy for example, it is best if you can identify which plant it is from, although you can also work with pollen generally if you do not know.

COMMON ALLERGENS
Use this list of common allergens to build up a picture of which things you are sensitive or allergic to. Give yourself a score for each positive reaction indicating a sensitivity.

Introduced environmental allergens

fertilizer	glues
fungicides	paints
herbicides	solvents
industrial chemicals	varnishes
insecticides	electromagnetic radiation
exhaust fumes	

Environmental allergens

animal hair	human hair
feathers	mould
house dust	pollen
house dust mite	insect bites

Food allergens

alcohol	sugar
caffeine	wheat
corn	chocolate
dairy produce	tomatoes
soya	tea

Centre and balance yourself, check your 'Yes' response, and dowse if it is appropriate and timely to dowse for allergens. If 'Yes', dowse down the list above or one you have written, resting a finger on each item and asking: 'Am I allergic or sensitive to this?' Make a separate list of all the items where your dowsing indicates that you have a sensitivity.

Desensitization strategies
It is often the case that a small handful of triggering allergens have a central destabilizing effect on our immune system, and that if we concentrate on and remedy these, the others will diminish to a level that the body can accommodate.

Dowse down your list of allergens asking: 'Is this a significant triggering allergen for me?' and make a new list of these. Typically at this stage you will have between one and five key allergens.

There are two strategies for working with allergens. One is by avoiding contact with the allergen which can be as easy as making a change in our diet or using a different detergent. Often the allergen is an unavoidable part of our environment, however, and avoidance is not always practical.

The other method involves reprogramming our immune system so that it learns to relate to the allergen in a normal and appropriate way. It is a bit like learning a new response to phobias.

For each of the triggering allergens, we aim to find a desensitizing number. This number represents a dilution at which our immune system can meet the allergen without experiencing an overload. The greater the triggering potential of an allergen, the more we need to dilute it to comfortably encounter it. This desensitizing number may be any number, but is often between 100 and 200.

Dowse a number for each allergen. Use 'More than...?' and 'Less than...?' dowsing questions to get the number for each allergen. Ask: 'Is the desensitizing number for house dust more than 100?' 'No.' 'More than 50?' 'Yes.' 'Less than 75?' 'Yes' and so on until you have the exact number.

Once you have all your numbers, sit peacefully and hold the thought of the allergen and its desensitizing number in your mind. Think of each one for a few minutes, 2 or 3 times each day for a week. You can dowse to find out exactly how often and for how long you should do this.

After a week, dowse the numbers again. The desensitizing number typically gets lower – quickly at first and then more slowly over further weeks, until it stabilizes or the allergen no longer has the capacity to trigger your immune system.

Dowse every so often to check which of the allergens on your triggering list you need to continue to work with and to update their numbers. Continue the practice for at least two weeks and then assess. You may find that you can eventually take some allergens off your list. It is very important that you do not take any health risks with allergens and their potential to harm you, but you might be surprised by dowsing's power.

Healthy aromas

An active sense of smell seems to have developed early on in our human evolution. One area in which most of us do still use smell in a primary way is in our relationship with food, which is a basic and essential survival skill for all animals.

Smells and our well-being

Most of the time, smell acts as background information, adding a layer of texture to our world, and influencing not so much our thoughts but our feelings and general sense of well-being. Although subliminal, this effect can be profound, rather like background music, which can influence our mood and level of activity even if it is playing quietly.

Many smells are cues for behavioural responses or are associated with particular places and activities. Take for example the smell of a forest or the ocean, of a petrol station or home-baking, of our working environment – these places each have their own particular smell, and give a cue to our body to wake up, go to sleep, be alert or perform in a particular way.

Some smells have a universal quality in the way that they influence people. Scents are used in spiritual practices to engage the mind in peaceful contemplation and to invoke particular qualities of spirit. Others are used in perfumes for their alluring or aphrodisiac qualities.

▼ Flowers help to cleanse and vitalize the air as well as adding their own fragrance and personality.

USING AROMATHERAPY OILS
In a diffuser or burner: 3 to 4 drops in water to scent a room.
Added to a bath: 4 to 6 drops – but mix them in 5ml/1 tsp of cream or full-cream milk first to help them disperse in the water.
For massage: the oils should be diluted in a massage oil (known as a 'carrier' or base oil). Light oils such as sweet almond or sunflower seed are ideal for use as a base oil. Use 3 drops of essential oil to 5ml/1 tsp of massage oil.
By inhalation: 1 to 2 drops in a bowl of hot water.
For localized pain: use hot or cold compresses, soaked in water containing 3 to 4 drops of oil. Squeeze the cloth out then apply.

The scents of plants are present in oils that the plant creates, and can be extracted in a highly concentrated form. These are called aromatic, or essential oils. Because of their profound effects upon us, plant aromas can be used as agents of balance and healing.

Aromatic oils for health

Aromatic oils are known to have been used for healing for thousands of years, and are currently enjoying great popularity.

Most commonly, essential oils are used in a diffuser or burner, added to a bath, or used in massage. Their effects are due to both their scent, and to the physiologically active compounds in the oil which are either inhaled or absorbed through the skin. Essential oils are concentrated substances with medicinal properties. They should be used sparingly – a few drops at a time. In general, aromatic oils are too strong to be used undiluted on the skin, although some oils, such as lavender, are gentle enough – but even then they should be used very sparingly. Other oils, because of their potency, could be harmful in certain conditions, including pregnancy. Aromatic oils should never be swallowed or taken internally.

DOWSING FOR AROMATIC OILS

Dowsing is a wonderful aid to guide you in selecting the most appropriate aromatic oils, whether for general well-being or to actively aid in a healing process. Start by asking the following questions: 'Would an aromatic oil be helpful in balancing and restoring my health at this time? Would a combination of aromatic oils be best?' If you find oils are suitable, then dowse over your selection of oils. If you have a large selection, you can save time by dividing the oils into two piles and ask: 'Do I need any of the oils in this pile?' Then you can ask: 'Is one drop of this oil sufficient? Two drops?' and so on until you find the right dosage.

1 Centre yourself, clear your mind and enter your state of alert, engaged non-attachment. Check your current signal for 'yes'. Having established that aromatic oils would benefit, dowse for your choice of oil.

2 For massage, add 3 drops of essential oil to at least 5ml/1 tsp of a carrier oil such as sweet almond oil, sunflower seed oil or other light nut, seed or vegetable oil. For baths, add 4 to 6 drops diluted in full-cream milk.

3 For inhalation, add 2 drops to a bowl of hot water. To scent a room, add 4 drops in water to an aromatic oil burner. For a compress to treat localized pain add 3 drops to a bowl of water, soak a cloth, squeeze and apply.

ESSENTIAL OILS

These are some suggestions to start with; always check with the supplier or an aromatherapy reference for possible contra-indications. Then dowse to see which oils suit you best.

Chamomile *Anthemis nobilis*
Soothing and calming, an antidepressant. Pain-killing, anti-inflammatory and antispasmodic. Good for muscle aches, inflamed joints, allergies and indigestion.

Bergamot *Citrus bergamia*
Uplifting, good for anxiety and shock. Antiseptic. Useful for oily, or infected skin. Acts as an appetite stimulant. Do not use before going into sunlight.

Lavender *Lavandula officinalis*
Calming and balancing, aids insomnia. Antidepressant. Pain-relieving. Helps wound healing, burns, insect bites and stings, aches and pains, and headaches.

Rose otto *Rosa otto*
Confidence-enhancing. Antidepressant. Aphrodisiac. Tones circulation and digestion. Helps dry skin. Helps regulate menstrual cycle, a powerful uterine tonic. Do not use in the first 4 months of pregnancy.

Rosemary *Rosmarinus officinalis*
Stimulant. Tonic for nervous system, heart, liver and gall bladder. Relieves muscular aches and pains, respiratory problems, colds, catarrh, sinusitis. Avoid in cases of epilepsy or high blood pressure; not to be used in the first 5 months of pregnancy.

Tea tree *Melaleuca alternifolia*
Immunostimulant. Antibacterial, antiviral and antifungal. Useful for acne, cold sores, and blisters of shingles and chicken pox. Good for catarrh and sinusitis. Used for warts, verrucas and athlete's foot (apply undiluted, but sparingly).

Flower essences

There is a philosophy that our natural environment has and always will provide us with everything that we need to restore and maintain our health in body, mind and spirit.

In 1930 Dr Edward Bach, an eminent English physician, left his flourishing homeopathic practice in London's Harley Street to pursue his ideal of bringing a simple system of healing within the reach of everyone. Believing that the divine light from which all humans could derive healing was particularly present in the energies of plants, he turned to the flowers of his native land to find remedies for the psychological and spiritual imbalances which he believed to be the cause of all illness. He was encouraged to do this by his own experience:

▼ Plants have a spirit or vital essence which is most strongly expressed in their flowers. The human emotional body is quickly affected by flower essences, and can receive healing from them.

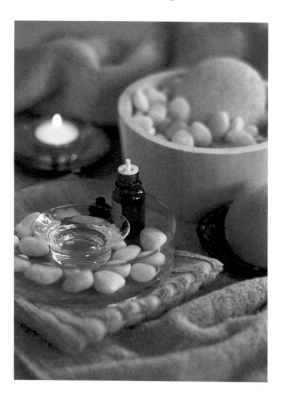

he had suffered physical illness and imbalances of both spirit and mind, and had healed himself by finding the relevant flower remedy. He went on to discover 38 remedies in all (often referred to as essences), which are still available today.

Vibrational patterns

Although not a dowser, Dr Bach worked in a highly intuitive way with plants. His approach differed from herbalism, where physiologically active constituents of plants are extracted for use in a concentrated form, and also from homeopathy, in which small amounts of an active substance is diluted many times over. Dr Bach's focus instead was on the very essence of the plant – its vibrational character or spirit – which he found to be most intensely present in its flowers. His theory was that all plants have a spirit or vital essence which is most strongly expressed in the flowers.

Bach then discovered that the plant's character could be absorbed as a vibrational pattern by water, and he began by collecting sun-drenched dew from freshly opened flowers. Later he found it was more practical to suspend freshly cut flowers in water for a few hours on a sunny day, and was just as effective. In this way, it seems that the vibrational qualities of the plant are transferred to the water and held as a memory pattern. These vibrations then become available when small amounts of the water – even just a few drops at a time – are ingested. The drops can be taken directly onto the tongue or mixed with a drink.

Bach or flower essences seem to work by influencing our subtle bodies – primarily the emotional body – with consequent healing and balancing effects upon the physical body through the spirit-mind-body connection. Because their influence is not through direct action on the physical body, and because they contain no physiologically active ingredients, the flower essences are safe and non-toxic to use.

Note: The base of the flower essence is often alcohol. If you have a sensitivity to alcohol choose one that has a water or a vinegar base.

DOWSING FOR NATURE'S HEALERS

Flower essences are among the most useful, safe and friendly ways to restore health and well-being. They work first on our emotions, with subsequent effects on the total body-mind-spirit entity. Powerful yet very gentle, they are safe to use at home for treating yourself, friends and family. Using dowsing to guide their selection and correct dosage allows us to get the best possible results from using them.

1 Begin by dowsing whether flower essences would be helpful for dealing with a current concern. Centre yourself and clear your mind, entering into a state of engaged non-attachment. Set your pendulum into its search position and check to confirm your 'Yes' signal.

Holding your issue or concern clearly in your mind, ask: 'Is it appropriate and timely for me to dowse for this?' If the answer is 'Yes', ask: 'Would flower essences be helpful and appropriate to use?' If the answer is 'Yes', then continue.

Dowse to find out which particular essence/s you need. If you already have a selection of essences, you can dowse from these. It is useful to have a full range of flower essences to choose from, but if you don't have the full set, you can dowse from a list or even take your pendulum with you when shopping.

2 When you have found the remedy that you need, almost fill a 30ml/1fl oz bottle with spring or filtered water and add 5ml/1 tsp of brandy, whisky or vinegar. Dowse to find out how many drops of each remedy you need, and add them to your bottle.

Alternatively, for more acute conditions, you can add the drops of flower remedy directly into a glass of spring water. Dowse as before to find out how many drops you need.

3 When you are ready to take the remedy, dowse to find out how many drops to put in your glass of water. Then take small sips of your drink as required. Flower remedies can work very quickly; see if you notice any change in your mood after taking them.

Creating flower remedies

▲ Sometimes we can read the essence of a plant by observing which insects, birds or animals are attracted to it.

Since Dr Bach's creation of his first flower remedies, many others have been inspired to follow this path of healing and have developed their own range of flower remedies or essences. Increasingly popular with holistic therapists as well as for home use, there is now a wide and comprehensive variety of flower remedy ranges from around the world available, each one having its own particular personality. Your dowsing can help you to choose which range is most suited to your needs.

Wherever we live however, nature will provide us with all that we need for health and balance and it is quite likely that the plants you need for your own healing may already be growing somewhere near you, perhaps in your garden or on wild land nearby. To create your own remedies from local sources is a wonderful way to both take an active interest in your health and to deepen your relationship with your environment. At the same time, the process of finding the flowers will open a channel for meditation and psychic discovery.

All living things on earth have not only a material, physical form, but one which is spiritual and invisible, and which has its own consciousness.

In the world of spirit, devas are the nature spirits responsible for the overall growth and health of plants. To discover which plants we need for our health and well-being, we first need to open up a channel to connect with the devic energies of the place where we are living.

Either in your garden, or wherever you feel most drawn to connect with the devas, create a time for quiet meditation, bringing your pendulum with you. You may choose a field, a wood, an open plain, or even your own garden. Wherever it is, find a comfortable spot, ideally where you can sit relaxed with your spine erect.

Centre yourself, clear your mind, and visualize yourself in a column of golden light, supported and protected by your own spirit guides.

When you feel peaceful and balanced, ask clearly in your mind to connect with the deva responsible for plant growth in that area. You may experience visual images or a sense of warmth and peace, it is different for each person, but you will know when you have made a connection.

Now begin dowsing. Set your pendulum into its neutral swing and check your 'Yes' signal. State clearly in your mind: 'I wish to ask about making flower remedies from local plants. Is it timely and appropriate to dowse about this?' If the answer is 'No', give thanks for the connection and try again at another time.

Choosing the right flowers

If the answer is 'Yes', then dowse to ask which flowers you can use and what their healing properties are. You may wish to search specifically for a plant or plants that will help with an existing concern that you have.

Be careful to frame your questions so that 'Yes' and 'No' are complete answers, and be open to ideas and suggestions that may occur to you as you proceed. Your intuition will give you information in every way that it can.

Start with a few different plants (not more than three), that your dowsing guides you to work with. Sit with each of these plants quietly and connect with the spirit of each one, noticing what images and feelings come to you. Check any ideas that you get with your dowsing, and find out as much as you can about how the plant will be helpful. If at any time you feel uncertain or insecure, check your 'Yes' response, and then dowse: 'Is it appropriate and timely for me to continue with this process?' Sometimes we need to proceed with small steps.

MAKING A FLOWER REMEDY

Once you have identified the right plant/s for you, the next step is to harvest freshly opened blossoms on a sunny day. Asking for help and guidance from the devas and also from the spirit of the individual plant, dowse to ask how many blossoms you need to take. This will depend on how much remedy you intend to make and the size and potency of the blossoms. The finished essence is best stored in dark bottles, but is stable at room temperature and can be kept without losing its properties almost indefinitely. For 0.5 litre/1 pint of flower remedy, up to seven flower blossoms would be typical. Cut the blossoms so that they fall into a glass bowl, ideally without handling them in the process. Add water, about two-thirds of the total volume of essence that you wish to make, and enough so that the blossoms are floating. Place the bowl in sunlight.

1 Direct your loving attention to the bowl, holding your hands over the water as though blessing it, while clearly asking in your mind that the energy of the blossoms be transferred into the water. Dowse to ask how long to add your own energy to the water and also how long to leave the bowl in sunlight. Once dowsing indicates the process is complete, give thanks to the spirit of the plant and remove the blossoms using a pair of clean tweezers.

2 Taking care not to touch the water with your hands as this may disturb and alter the flower essence, pour the water into a clean glass jar and add vinegar or spirit-strength alcohol (brandy or whisky are ideal) to stabilize and sterilize the remedy. Add about half as much vinegar or alcohol as water, place the lid on the jar and keep in a cool, dark place. This is your stock solution from which you can make up dosing bottles as needed.

Enjoying life and finding your path

A fully healthy life is one where all aspects of oneself are appropriately energized, and where everything that we do is congruent with our core values and our sense of self.

Attaching value to the work that we do is an essential ingredient to cultivating emotional integrity and a sense of well-being. There is a story of a traveller encountering three men working on a building site, each one engaged with the same job. He asks them what they are doing. The first replies, 'Can't you see? I'm breaking rocks!' The second answers, 'Me? I'm earning a living to support my family.' The third pauses in his work and tells the traveller, 'I'm helping to build this cathedral to the glory of God.'

A wellness programme

Many of us drift along and only focus on issues of health when we feel something is wrong. Well-being and vibrant health are qualities that need to be consciously cultivated and not left to chance.

It is tempting to allow ourselves to become depleted through the week and then do something healthy at the weekend to make up the balance. Or perhaps we allow ourselves to get depleted through the year and hope to rectify the balance with a week or two of holiday. An alternative to this boom/bust cycle is to start to integrate health-giving activities into every day even if we believe we don't have enough time or our days are already full.

Begin by identifying everything you would need in your life to feel totally healthy and fully expressed. Take the time to draw up a list and put down everything that brings you joy and makes your heart sing. Include the things that are of central importance and value for yourself, family and community. Don't worry if the list gets long. Group them each into body, mind and spirit categories.

Now go through your list and see which items you give lots of energy to, and which ones are being starved of time and attention. You might also consider where most of your time and attention actually does go, is it to areas that are not on your list at all? Next, see if you can identify the core characteristics of the things that you love to do or feel good about doing. Whether the activities are at home, at work, in leisure or with the family, perhaps a common thread is being with people, or doing things as part of a team. Or perhaps being outdoors is the core component to several activities on your list. By looking through your list in this light, you can generate a smaller, stripped-down list of core qualities that are always present in the things that make your heart sing. List these as before under body, mind and spirit headings.

From threads to strong fabric

The second part of creating the wellness programme is to weave these core qualities into every part of your life. Simply by having a clear idea of what these central qualities are, will take you a long way towards prioritizing your time. Seek to include more of your core qualities in your existing

▼ Integrate the things which bring joy and pleasure into your life, rather than waiting for burn-out to tell you that something is wrong.

daily routine. As choices come up for you, consider how many of your core qualities are in each option. Look for ways to maximize your time by weaving activities together. If there are qualities that are not getting much time or attention, look to see why this is. It is possible that you have fears or difficulties around prioritizing them, that they seem out of reach or too self-indulgent. Look for ways that these neglected areas can be energized effortlessly and without disrupting the fabric of your life. Perhaps they can be expressed in something that you already do, or met in an easier way, or made part of your work or shared leisure time.

Dowsing with a wellness chart
Make a chart like the one shown here, covering each area of your life, or use this basic one to begin with. Set your pendulum swinging backwards and forwards so that it swings into the inner neutral area. Now ask the question: 'Which area of my life do I most need to focus my attention on to enhance my health and well-being?' The pendulum will continue to swing, but will change the direction of its swing to point to one of the wedges of the chart. You might do this two or three times, asking: 'Which is the next most important area

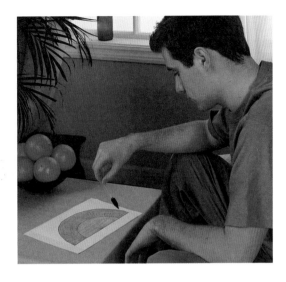

▲ Once you engage with the practice, you will find yourself making increasingly healthy choices.

of my life to focus my attention on to enhance my health and well-being?' With this information, dowse further into each of the topic areas identified. Let your spirit guide you in making healthy choices and finding healthy solutions from the options available to you.

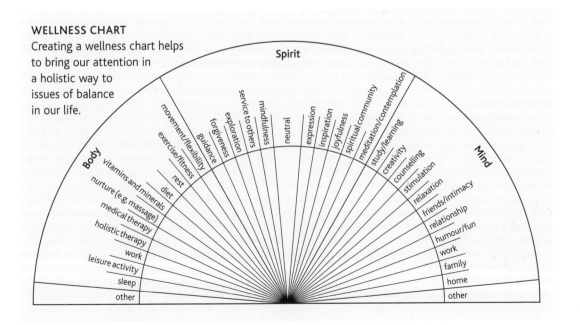

WELLNESS CHART
Creating a wellness chart helps to bring our attention in a holistic way to issues of balance in our life.

Vital Healing

'Your intelligence is always with you,
overseeing your body, even though
you may not be aware of its work.
If you start doing something against
your health, your intelligence
will eventually scold you.'

RUMI (1207–1273)

The healing gift

One of the great human gifts and mysteries is our ability to channel healing energy, if the need is present and if we open ourselves to do so. What could be more natural than to comfort a child who has fallen during play and hold the place that hurts, even to kiss it better? It is hard to say exactly what exchange has taken place, but the outcome is that the child feels reassured and comforted, and the acute distress and often the pain itself disappears. The body may take some time afterwards to heal itself, but it seems as though, at a subtle energetic level, a healing exchange has already occurred, and the child's psychic and emotional energy becomes directed elsewhere as it returns to play.

Healing is an entirely natural expression of the human spirit, bringing grace and balance to both the channel and the recipient of that energy. It is often associated with a deeply peaceful feeling of engaged compassion. Healing can be practised quite spontaneously and intuitively, or it can be focused through structured and systematized techniques. No one method of healing is necessarily better than another, what is important is to heal in a way that feels natural and comfortable for you as an individual. There are no rules to follow when healing, but there are a few helpful guide-

▲ The human desire to comfort and heal is one of the most natural and basic of our instincts, and powerfully affirms our fundamental nature.

lines to bear in mind, particularly for people who find a vocation in healing and become intensely or frequently engaged with it. Adhering to these guidelines will help healing to occur.

GUIDELINES FOR HEALING

• Research and experience shows that true healing works best when we project energy in a completely unconditional form and are unattached to the outcome. Simply channelling unconditional, loving energy to another person supports their spirit in finding wholeness and balance in whatever way is right for them.

• When giving healing, see yourself as a channel through which healing energy can pass, rather than seeing it as coming directly from you. When you are healing, ask that you too may benefit through the process.

• Remain unattached to the outcome of your healing activity, and don't judge the results. This seems strange as one might expect a successful outcome to always be a complete physical recovery from an illness or injury. However, we cannot know or judge the path of another's spirit through the world.

• Be unattached to the nature of the illness or injury of your subject. Whatever we focus our attention upon, we give strength to, and invite into our own lives. When transferring energy hold your focus on the unconditional love that you are channelling.

The healing sequence

Ask first: 'Is it appropriate and timely for me to be channelling healing energy for (name)?' If the answer is 'Yes', put down your pendulum for a moment, and visualize yourself in a column of golden light. Invite healing energy to enter you from the source of healing and love. Some people feel the energy in their hands as heat or perhaps other sensations, and others feel little or nothing, but the healing works just as well either way.

Returning to your pendulum, dowse for the optimum positioning of your hands for directing the healing energy. Ask questions such as: 'Are my hands needed where the pain is? Around the heart area? Is this the best position now?' and so on, until you find where your hands need to go. You can dowse to find out whether your hands should be directly in contact or a little apart.

Once you have found the position, relax and visualize unconditional, loving energy flowing into you, through you, and out of your hands into and all around your subject. You may spontaneously feel when it is time to move your hands; use your dowsing at intervals to confirm: 'Is there anywhere else that I should be channelling healing to? Is the process complete now?' Once finished, visualize that the energetic connection is ending and then that it has stopped. Visualize yourself filled with golden light, clean, clear, whole and healthy, and give thanks to the source of healing and love.

CHANNELLING HEALING ENERGY

To be effective in channelling healing energy it is important to pay attention to your own state of well-being. You will need to practice centring and opening yourself to the divine healing energy. Your intuition will tell you all that you need to know for healing effectively. In the presence of someone who has asked you for healing, centre yourself, clear your mind, and allow your body to be relaxed and alert.

1 Allow yourself to become calm and peaceful, centred and balanced, paying attention to your breathing. Invite healing energy into you from the source of healing and love, visualizing yourself inside a column of golden light.

2 You may notice a tingling or vitalizing sensation in your body or a kind of energy bubble between your hands. Move your hands as your feelings and your dowsing indicate, and allow healing energy to flow freely as it will.

3 You may both have a clear sense when the healing process is complete. Your dowsing will confirm this. Visualize the connection between you ending, imagine yourself clean and clear, whole and healthy, full of loving energy, and give thanks.

Channel of subtle energy

The spinal column is the central axis of our bony skeleton, and the spinal cord which it surrounds and protects is the central pathway of our nervous system. Additionally, important networks of nerves which co-ordinate and govern many of the body's autonomic activities are centrally placed in front of the spine, and the largest of our arteries and veins carrying blood to and from the heart, lie adjacent to the spine. The blood supply and the nerves radiate out from the spinal column, which is the central axis of our physical and spiritual well-being.

A conduit for information exchange, nerve fibres enter and exit our spine, bringing information to and from widespread and corresponding parts of the whole body, co-ordinating the many interdependent systems that work synergistically together. Therapists working with spinal injury understand the far-reaching consequences that damage to the spine will have.

▼ Just as the seeds of this plant radiate outwards, and then outwards again, so the nerves leave the spine and connect with all parts of the body, down to the single cell.

The subtle body

As well as having a physical body composed of matter, we also have a subtle or energy body which consists of vibrational frequency. The subtle body is believed to be an energy field in and around the physical body that holds the pattern and form (inspired by the vital essence or spirit) upon which the material framework of the physical body is organized. This subtle, vibrational body co-exists with and interpenetrates the physical body, and is constantly exchanging information and energy with it.

When any physical injury or illness occurs, an associated and equivalent vibrational imbalance or trauma in the subtle body is also present. It is believed that the healing energies which we channel are of the same vibrational frequency as the subtle body, and that they are absorbed and integrated first by it rather than by the physical body.

During any healing process, health and balance is understood to return to the subtle body first, either through its own healing processes or in an accelerated and enhanced fashion through the channelling of healing energy from another source. Once the vibrational pattern is restored, the physical body then returns to health at its own, slightly slower pace.

Identical to its physical counterpart, the subtle body also has the spine as its central axis, the focal point of balance and the centre of organization and information exchange. When studying the subtle body, it is often perceived as having several layers extending outwards from the physical body, or of consisting of several separate but interwoven subtle bodies which are arranged on the physical body concentrically.

Different traditions give these subtle bodies (or the subtle body's layers) different names and describe them in slightly different terms. One version is that there are seven in number, including the physical, all centred upon the spine. Each one is somewhat larger and of a higher vibration than the previous one, and each is associated with a different level of consciousness. The smallest and

THE CHAKRA SYSTEM

The seven levels of human consciousness are represented by energetic nodal points along our vertical axis. In the Hindu tradition these are termed chakras, assigned to points of the body, and to specific colours.

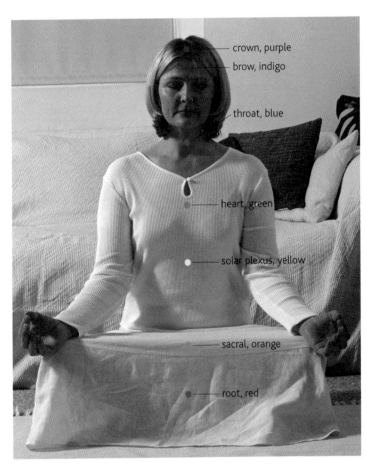

crown, purple
brow, indigo
throat, blue
heart, green
solar plexus, yellow
sacral, orange
root, red

▲ One way of imaging the subtle body is through the use of Kirlian photography. This technique creates a picture of the parts of the vibrational energy field nearest to the physical plane – those energies concerned with holding the physical and emotional pattern and form.

most dense is the level of the physical body and the largest and most refined is the level at which we become one with the source of love and healing, or the Divine.

The seven chakras

As well as the seven vibrational layers or levels radiating outwards from the spine, it is also considered that there are seven nodal points where energy is focused (generally referred to as the chakras), arranged along the length of the spine, which similarly have resonance with different levels of our consciousness. This reinforces our understanding that the spine is not only the central core of our energetic anatomy but is also a channel of access which allows us to reach every little part of the whole.

However one may see this, the key for us when engaging in healing is that by holding the spine as our central focus, we can simultaneously channel healing energy to every level and part of the body.

Here at the centre of the body, all levels are equally present, and balance and health restored in one level will facilitate the return of balance and health in each of the others, body, mind and spirit. Truly a divine path for healing.

Healing through the spine

▲ Like the tree and waterfall, energy in the spine moves from sources below and from sources above.

We know now how to call on healing energies and how to channel them through our hands. We are also familiar with the spine as a key focus for directing our healing attention.

In the presence of someone who has asked you to channel healing energy for them, begin by centring yourself and clear your mind. Allow your body to be relaxed and alert. Set your pendulum swinging in neutral, and ask if it is appropriate and timely for you to be channelling healing energy for this person. If you receive a 'Yes' response, visualize yourself in a column of golden light, and invite healing energy to enter you from the source of healing and love.

Next, ask of your dowsing whether your healing should first be directed towards the spine. If you receive a 'No', follow your intuition and ask further questions of your dowsing to find out where to put your hands. Once you feel and have confirmed with your dowsing that sufficient energy has been

transferred there, ask again if you should now focus on the spine. If 'No', continue to find the next hand position. You may find you complete the session without ever having focused on the spine.

When your intuition and dowsing say to bring your attention to the spine, begin by asking whether your hands will be together over the same place. If 'Yes' then you have only one spinal level to find. If 'No' then you have two spinal levels to find.

You now need to find the correct positions for your hands. To do this, move your dowsing hand slowly down the spine, asking to be shown where to place it. Use your middle finger as a pointer when you get close to the exact level. Apply your other hand in the same way, and visualize the transfer of loving, healing energy while allowing yourself to remain engaged, compassionate and unattached. This process of finding the correct spinal level can be quite quick once you are familiar with it and many people find that they can sense the right level intuitively, only relying on dowsing for confirmation or checking their accuracy.

After a while you will feel that the energy is slowing down. This could be the moment to move on or to end the session. Use dowsing to confirm that sufficient energy has been transferred to the spinal level where you are working, and then dowse to find out if there is more to do elsewhere (and if so where to direct the energy), or if the session is over. When your dowsing indicates that you are finished, visualize the energetic connection between you and your subject ending and stopping. Visualize that you are entirely filled with golden light, clean, clear, whole and healthy, and give thanks to the source of healing, light and love.

Conclude by dowsing to see if a further session is needed, and if so when the best time would be.

SCANNING THE SPINE

To most effectively focus our healing through the spine we need to know at which level the energy can be most easily absorbed and have the greatest benefit. Dowsing offers guidance at each part of the process.

1 Begin with your subject sitting comfortably, try and put them at their ease. Start your pendulum swinging in neutral and hold your free hand out with an open palm, a few inches from their body. Start with your hand at the level of the very top of their head, and, without ever physically touching them, scan progressively downwards, following the line of their spine all the way down the centre of their back from their head, down their neck, mid-back and lower back until you reach the level of their tail bone at the bottom.

2 As you do this, hold clearly in your mind the question: 'Is this where I should place my left/right hand?' (depending on which is the free scanning hand). As you go, you will find at some point that your pendulum starts to swing into its 'Yes' response. To get the exact level, go over the approximate area again, starting just a little above where your 'Yes' response began, but moving more slowly down the spine this time and pointing with a finger. If you hold your pendulum close to your scanning finger, you will find it easier.

3 Next ask your dowsing if your hand should be placed on the person's physical body. If 'Yes', place your hand against their spine, covering the indicated spot with the centre of your palm. If 'No', start with your open hand next to the spine and slowly bring it outwards until your pendulum indicates the appropriate distance.

Spinal dowsing

We have discovered that the physical and subtle bodies share their central core in the spine, and that they constantly exchange energy and information. We have also seen that imbalances in the pattern of the subtle, vibrational body can manifest in the matter of the physical body.

One place where imbalances are commonly exchanged and shared is between the levels of the mental, emotional and physical bodies. When an unresolved issue is triggered (such as a particular fear for example) by an event, memory or such like, the mind may interpret incoming information as overwhelming, and instead of processing and

▼ Bringing gentle, loving energy to areas which have been traumatized, whether physically or emotionally, helps the process of healing to occur.

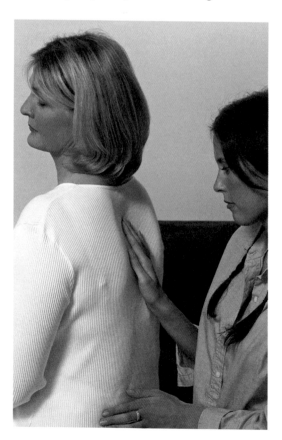

releasing the emotional energy created, it simply transfers it to the physical body which contains and protects it by contracting around it and walling it off. By observing a person's posture, you can recognize the emotional holding patterns which gradually and progressively influence and overshadow their basic character and personality. Gentle healing for body, mind and spirit releases the mental and emotional tension and allows the person to return to their original, natural posture.

The compromised posture can impair many different systems, including the critical nerves that enter and exit the spine at the affected level. Working directly at the physical level where the imbalance is stored, the posture of the spine can be gently helped to correct itself and the postural muscles on either side of the spine encouraged to release the knots. This aids a return to normal function, including that of the related nerves and associated information channels.

In the process of restoring the physical body to greater flexibility and natural balance, intensely emotional memories may surface of the original hurt which has been stored in the body, and through emotional release the person is brought to a sense of deep peace and healing. Holding a safe space while this emotional unburdening occurs is an important and key part of the healing process.

Restoring flexibility

You can help the spine to regain its natural state of balance by using dowsing to reconnect with the tight shut-down places, to restore energy flow and flexibility and allow the spine to remember its most healthy posture.

First check the 'Yes' response of your pendulum and then, in the presence of someone who has asked you for healing, dowse whether it is timely and appropriate to channel healing for them. If the answer is 'Yes', then ask if they have any known disease or injury of their spine. If they are not sure, you can check with the pendulum. (If they do, however, it is best to channel healing energy to the appropriate area of the subtle body and not directly to the physical one.) Having checked it's safe to work directly on the spine, ask your dowsing whether helping their spine to adjust its posture is timely and appropriate. If 'Yes', scan slowly down the spine from the crown to the tailbone as before, asking in your mind: 'Please show me the fulcrum point for the necessary postural adjustment.'

When you have found the right place, put down your pendulum and place your thumbs gently against the spine, one on either side. Now, while keeping your thumbs in place, invite your subject to gently, in their own time and without going beyond their comfortable range of motion, go through four simple movements described below.

DOWSING THE SPINE

Start with your subject sitting comfortably relaxed with their spine straight and tall, breathing slowly and deeply. Then invite them to perform the following movements. The size and range of movements is not important; these should be done gently and slowly and feel entirely comfortable to your subject. Do not let them strain, hurt or over-extend themselves. The gentle touch of your thumbs will call their spine to an awareness of that level and give it the necessary information to direct appropriate healing there. A combination of gentle postural adjustment, massage and healing guided by dowsing is a tremendously effective way to restore health and balance to the central axis of our physical and subtle bodies.

1 Ask your subject to arch her back around where she feels the touch of your fingers, and then return to upright.

2 Then ask her to bend forwards and in so doing pushing your fingers backwards, and then return to upright.

3 She then rotates to the right, turning to look over the right shoulder, then back to upright. This is repeated to the left.

▶ **4** After the spinal movements, dowse to see if there is another postural adjustment required, and if so follow the same procedure as before. You may find only one to be necessary or perhaps several. Now dowse to see if gentle massage is required to help soften the holding pattern of the muscles. If indicated, massage in small circles into the large muscles immediately to each side of the spine. You will feel these gradually soften and let go under your fingers. Dowse to see where and for how long this should be done. Finally, dowse to see if channelling healing energy to the subtle body is also required. If 'Yes', proceed with this as before until the session is complete.

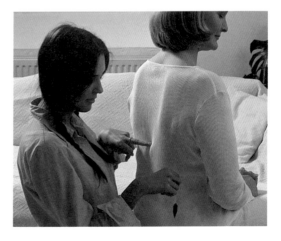

Healing through hands and feet

We have discovered that healing energy can be directed to a number of different levels, and that the interconnection between the subtle and physical bodies can allow indirect as well as direct attention to be brought effectively to areas of imbalance and impaired health.

Reflexology is a gentle and non-invasive healing technique which is easy to learn and safe to use and can be guided entirely by dowsing. It is based on the understanding that there are subtle energetic connections between the hands and feet and all other parts of the body, including the internal organs and their related physiological systems. A form of holographic map of the body is laid out on both hands and feet, each side of the body being mapped out on the corresponding hand and foot.

By stimulating the appropriate part of the hand or foot, an energetic transfer is effected to the related point in the body.

Reflexologists use their knowledge of these maps and their related points to focus their healing attention and also to help them in diagnosing areas of concern, even before these have shown up as physical problems. We can also use these energetic associations, allowing our dowsing to guide us.

Dowsing the hands and feet

In the presence of your subject, centre yourself and clear your mind, and with your body relaxed and alert start your pendulum in its neutral swing and check your 'Yes' response. Ask if it is appropriate and timely for you to be channelling

ZONES ON THE FEET

This diagram depicts the reflexology zones running along the feet. The two big toes also represent the whole head. The right side of your body lies on your right foot, and the left side of your body is correspondingly positioned on the left foot.

ZONES ON THE BODY

Diaphragm line

Waist line

Pelvis/Heel line

Linking zones run vertically through the body, from head to feet and hands. There are also transverse lines which correspond with the reflex areas on the feet.

▲ Dowse to find the reflexology points on the hand or foot which require your attention.

▲ Apply firm but gentle pressure to the points indicated for 10 to 20 seconds, then re-check.

healing energy for the person. If 'Yes', ask if it is most appropriate to focus your healing through reflexology. If 'Yes' again, ask your subject whether they would prefer you to work on their hands or on their feet. If working on their feet, they will need to remove their shoes and socks.

Before you start, visualize yourself in a column of golden light and invite healing energy to enter you from the source of healing and love.

Begin with the right hand or foot. Start by simply holding it until the level of intimacy feels comfortable and relaxed. Then place the thumb of your non-dowsing hand against the sole of the foot or the palm of the hand and begin dowsing.

With your pendulum in its neutral swing, state clearly in your mind: 'I wish to channel healing energy through the reflex zones of this hand/foot. Please guide me to where healing is most needed.'

Then begin a series of directional questions to guide your thumb to its first point. 'Is the first point to the left of where my thumb is? To the right? Nearer to the toes/fingers? At each point, direct firm but gentle pressure inwards with your thumb while visualizing a transfer of loving energy. Apply pressure steadily for several seconds, then release and reapply. Don't dig in with your nail.

Dowse after about 20 seconds to find out if sufficient energy has been transferred. If it has, ask if there is another point for you to work on. You may be guided back to a point a second time.

Continue until your dowsing indicates that you are finished with that foot or hand. Hold it in a supportive way to complete your interaction with it, then transfer to the left hand or foot.

When the session is complete, visualize the end of the energetic transfer, and fill yourself with golden energy which is clear, whole and healthy. Give thanks to the source of love and healing.

FOOT CHART

These diagrams indicate the linkages between the foot and the rest of the body. With dowsing specific knowledge of these areas isn't necessary; simply let your dowsing and intuition guide you to the points.

Absent healing

We can dowse for something that is not physically present with us, and we can send healing energy to a person who is somewhere else at the time. We can only speculate about why this is so, it would appear that at the level of spirit, there is a unified energy field that allows us to perceive and interact with all things simultaneously. Whatever the reason, it is familiar and accepted practice for healers and dowsers to not only work with their subjects when they are physically present but also to work with them when they are somewhere else.

This presents a wonderful opportunity. Either by using a natural period of quiet time that occurs during our day, or by setting time aside that we can be sure will be peaceful and uninterrupted, we can focus healing energy on friends and loved ones in need, wherever they may be and whatever they may be doing. Similarly, we can extend our practice to any number of people who have requested healing from us. Many healers maintain an absent-healing list, communicating with people until healing has occurred and health has been restored again.

▲ When sending healing, visualize your subject filled and surrounded by healing, loving energy. Be unconditional and unattached to the outcome of your healing. It is not always possible to know what outcome is best for each person's spiritual path.

▼ Set time aside in a place where you can enter a quiet and meditative state without being disturbed. Lighting a candle provides a focus and creates a peaceful atmosphere.

Performing absent healing

Begin by creating a peaceful setting for yourself where you will not be disturbed. Some people like to create an altar space to help relax and focus the mind, the presence of a candle, some flowers, and perhaps some incense to assist in focusing your mind towards loving and healing thoughts. Have your pendulum to hand.

Having settled yourself, focus for a while on your breathing and allow yourself to become peaceful and relaxed. Ask for guidance, support and protection from the source of love and healing. State clearly in your mind that you wish to perform absent healing, and visualize yourself sitting in a column of golden light, completely energized, clear and balanced. Dowsing with your pendulum, ask if you are ready to start absent healing. If the answer is a clear 'Yes', then you can proceed. If it is a 'No' or qualified by a 'But...' check to see if you are fully centred. It may be that you are not in the right frame of mind to be doing absent healing, or it may be that the timing is not right for some other reason. Take more time to relax and centre yourself, and then ask again. If your dowsing still tells you not to proceed, then leave for another time.

Before you can send distant healing, you need to tune-in to the recipient. This is rather like giving a dog a piece of clothing that someone has worn so that it may follow their scent. We need to pick up the scent of our subject. Some healers do this using a photograph or a piece of the person's hair. Others are content with a name and address, perhaps with a birth date and any other personal details that will help to uniquely identify that person. For people that we know well, we can often tune-in simply by thinking of them.

▼ Absent healing is simple and powerful. As well as helping individuals in need, we can send unconditional healing love to places and situations.

As you tune-in, dowse to see if it is appropriate and timely to be sending them absent healing. If the answer from your pendulum is 'Yes', begin to send unconditional love to them. A simple visualization of that person surrounded by and in a column of golden light works beautifully. Do not be distracted by anything that you know about the person or their concerns, and do not hold any attachment or judgement to the process, or the outcome.

Hold the image in your mind for a minute or two or until you feel complete. Dowse to see if more energy is needed. If not, move on to the next person to whom you wish to send absent healing. Between each person, focus for a few moments on your own breathing and re-visualize yourself in your own column of golden light, in which you are energized, balanced and healthy. After healing you should feel refreshed, calm and healthy, if you do not, seek help from someone more experienced.

When you have finished the session, fill yourself with loving energy and let go of the energetic attachments to others. Visualize yourself clear, balanced and whole and give thanks to the source of love and healing.

Earth Energies

'Every continent has its own great spirit of place. Every people is polarized in some particular locality, which is home, the homeland. Different places on the face of the earth have different vital effluence, different vibration, different chemical exhalation, different polarity with different stars: call it what you like, but the spirit of place is a great reality.'

D H LAWRENCE (1885–1930)

The spirit of place

Having developed an awareness of the connection between body, mind and spirit, and gained an understanding that the subtle body holds the intrinsic energy field for the denser physical body, the dowser can extend this perception to appreciate the subtle energy field present in all things.

Interconnectedness

The relationship between the subtle and physical body, or the interconnectedness between spirit and matter, applies equally well to trees and plants, to birds and fish, even to rocks and rivers, as it does to human beings. The etheric layer of the subtle body, that is, the level closest to the physical body, is the western equivalent of the eastern chi or qui (pronounced chee), and is present in all things, albeit at different levels. It holds the vibratory energy field and gives both pattern and form to physical matter.

Places of character and personality

We are all familiar with places that seem special to us. Whether a corner of our garden, a forest clearing or an awe-inspiring mountain top, each of us has been touched by the special and individual qualities of places that we know or have visited.

Often, our experience of visiting these places is similar to that of spending time with a dear and close friend, and our emotions are touched. We can feel inspired or calmed for example by our encounter with a particular spot, and may even describe the character of the place in very human terms: we speak of places as being warm and friendly, or cold and hostile, peaceful and serene, or disturbed and restless. Although these terms can be applied to the literal, physical characteristics of the place, we are more usually describing our experience of that place, how it made us feel, rather than what it was actually like. It's something we experience more in

▼ Being still and offering our imagination to the landscape allows us to experience its subtle nature more fully. This creates harmony and balance within and can give a wonderful sense of well-being and contentedness. A little time spent in this way is valuable to everyone.

our stomach and heart rather than in our head. In these cases, we are describing our encounter with the spirit of place.

Humans have intensely developed mental and emotional energy. We have the capacity for self-reflection and the ability to exercise free will. However, our energy body is tiny in comparison to that of our surroundings.

We are all familiar with the way in which our mood is gradually influenced by the tone of music playing in the background. Similarly, our moods and thoughts and many of the circumstances that we take for granted and react to in our daily lives, are defined and patterned by the background, ambient energy field of the place in which we find ourselves. The energy field of place has enormous psychic mass and presence.

Clearly, our relationship with the spirit of place is inevitable and ever-present and is perhaps our most primary and defining relationship. Certainly as we explore issues of personal health, and examine our relationship with every part of who we are and what we do, the relationship we have with place, whether healthy or unhealthy, is one which has immense impact and importance in our life.

The spirit of environmentalism

Our awareness of environmental issues, including resource limitation, water, air and soil, sound, light pollution and issues of biodiversity, is now creating many and far-reaching changes in cultural attitudes and behaviour towards the planet.

At the largest or broadest level, one could consider the vast energy field of the earth itself. This great energy spirit is often referred to as Gaia, the spirit of the planet, our home and hostess for the duration of our earthly life here.

At a purely basic level of survival, we have become increasingly aware that we are fouling our nest. Much of the thinking of the environmental movement, however, comes from the same material consciousness that has created the current problems, and even wilderness areas are seen in terms of recreational or aesthetic resources, possibly containing plant species that can be exploited for human medicines or cosmetics. Also, such places are designated special and different, and although

▲ Each day, we are in constant and intimate contact with the earth, whether we are conscious of it or not, exchanging not only air, water and food but also etheric, emotional and mental energy.

we may take care of these, we have less regard for other, supposedly less significant places.

Sustainability is now seen to be essential, but we are sometimes approaching it in material, technological and economic terms, many of which are fundamentally incompatible with the very nature of sustainability itself. So-called primitive cultures have achieved sustainability for thousands of years in their landscapes, even in those areas that are farmed. If we cannot also achieve this, something is missing or wrong, in our approach.

If we were to hold this awareness of and respect for the spirit of place, the conclusions we would draw and our behaviour would be markedly different from those arising when an awareness of spirit is lacking. This applies equally, whether we are speaking at an individual or at a global level. Perhaps a central key to our short and long-term health therefore lies fundamentally in our relationship with, and our awareness and reverence for, the spirit of place.

The spirit of the earth

The anatomy of the earth's subtle body is a subject of great fascination, and an area where science and spirituality, folklore and legend meet. We can learn a great deal by comparing it with similar, but smaller energy bodies, such as that of a person.

Flowing chi

In Traditional Chinese Medicine (TCM) much attention is given to the flow and distribution of chi around the body. Chi is a Chinese word for subtle, etheric energy, and their understanding is that this is present in every part of the body, animating and vitalizing the physical structure. Practices such as t'ai chi cultivate and balance this energy, with great benefits to health and well-being.

While present throughout the body, chi is recognized to have its own circulatory system of meridian lines. These follow connective pathways and distribute chi to every part of the body.

Health suffers when one or more of these chi-paths becomes blocked and energy stagnates or, contrastingly, becomes over-stimulated, causing an excess of energy. The resulting imbalance becomes manifest in mind and body. To restore and maintain a healthy balance of chi, TCM works on nodal

▲ Nodal points on the web of the earth's subtle body have long been recognized as places of energetic focus, and are used to balance the fields of energy from the surrounding landscape.

points along the paths, where energetic input at these points can apply leverage to the path as a whole. Acupuncture is the practice of working upon these nodal points with needles.

Dragons in the landscape

Many people believe that this characteristic of chi circulation and distribution is fundamental to every energy system, including that of the earth. According to the Chinese the chi-paths of the earth's subtle body have traditionally been known as dragons.

Dragons inhabit every landscape. Typically described as having the body of a serpent, the scales of a fish, the wings of a bat and the claws of a bird, they symbolize the energy that is present in all animals and throughout nature. They bring the etheric energy through the land, making it available to serpent and fish, bat and bird.

Sinuous and mercurial by nature, their energies fluctuate and change with sunrise and sunset, with the waxing and waning of the moon, with the passing of the sun through the seasons and with the deep, quiet cycles of planetary time.

Nomadic cultures followed the seasonal rise and fall of energy in the landscape, knowing both the location of the nodal points on the dragon paths, and the times at which the intensified etheric energy at those places would be most active. As nomadic people began to settle and turn their attention to agriculture, they developed a more fixed relationship with the landscape, remaining in the same location all the year round. They then found it expedient to tame the local dragons, pinning them down and stabilizing their energy at the nodal points in order to heighten and balance the surrounding energies, so as to keep them throughout the year.

The legacy of this elegant technology is seen in the standing stones and stone circles of the British Isles and northern Europe, the pyramids of Egypt, the temples of ancient Greece, the sacred sites of Central and South America, in fact, all over the world where agriculture has flourished, the dragons have been tethered and cultivated. By contrast, in landscapes where the nomadic lifestyle has not been given up by the indigenous people, the power centres remain less worked by human hands, and the dragons continue to visit still of their own accord, on more seasonal terms.

This Chinese system is not the only system of energetic classification. The West recognizes its own dragons or energy lines, which are as old as those of the East and all are older than human classification. In addition to energy or ley lines of different magnitudes, which form more or less rectilinear grids across the earth, the form of the land and the geological characteristics below the surface all bear an influence. In addition, there are also energy paths for each of the elements: earth, air, fire and water.

Yin and yang chi

Drawing further on the traditional Chinese understanding of these elemental forces, we can begin to discern different kinds of dragons around us, and to become aware of their various qualities. We can start by observing yin chi-paths and yang

▲ The movement of water, both overground in rivers, and underground in natural aquifers, is central to the energetic anatomy of a landscape.

chi-paths. Yin and yang are not terms of absolute description, in the way that right and left or up and down are, rather they are terms of relative comparison, in the way that we would use more and less or higher and lower for example. Something with a yin nature is relatively quiet, receptive, of an absorbing, introspective nature. Something with a yang nature on the other hand, has a relatively active, expansive, penetrating and expressive quality.

Some chi-paths are by their nature yin, and others by their nature are yang. The Chinese make no distinction between human and landscape chi, and refer to the yin chi-path as the white tiger and the yang chi-path as the azure dragon in landforms.

Where the yin and yang chi-paths meet, particularly if this coincides with nodal points on one or both paths, then the etheric energy is most intensely present in a multiplied and interwoven form at that point. These places are known as power-centres, and are sites of intensified spiritual observance and practice.

Energy awareness

Knowing that we are surrounded by energy patterns of various kinds, it is good to have an awareness of the way in which they may affect us. Just as our health is related to the quality of food that we eat and the quality of the air that we breathe, human beings are exquisitely sensitive to the surrounding etheric energy field. Changes in our mood and energy level can be influenced by the predominant energy of our immediate environment. The effect of being in predominantly yin chi slows us down, rather like the glass of wine or heavy meal. Predominantly yang chi on the other hand, acts like coffee, stimulating and speeding us up. These effects increase with the intensity of the etheric field, and can be more extreme the more strongly the etheric field is polarized to yin or yang.

▼ Some locations naturally emanate a calming atmosphere of repose and tranquillity. We are often drawn towards them in times of stress.

This means that a high-intensity, highly polarized etheric field, such as that carried by a large dragon line of either yin or yang nature, will affect us much more and much more quickly than a low-intensity etheric field. Chi-paths that are small and relatively weak, are composed of more evenly balanced yin and yang energies.

Although affecting us mainly at a subtle energetic level, our mood, thoughts and physical energies are all coloured by the spirit of place due to the body-mind-spirit connection, with resulting influence on our health. Furthermore, the longer that we spend in any one place, the greater will be its effect upon us.

These effects can be good, bad or indifferent for a human, depending on how well matched we are to the places where we spend our time. Some places are more or less beneficial, and some particularly significant for individuals. By contrast, the subtle energy field of other places, or of particular areas within them, may be damaging and harmful.

▲ The health of plant and animal species that have similar energetic preferences to humans are good indicators of the nature of our environments.

Geopathic stress

The modern term used for stress on our health caused by earth energy is geopathic stress. This is not a new idea however. The Roman historian, Plutarch (*c*. 45–125CE) stated: 'Men are affected by streams of varying potency issuing from the Earth. Some of these drive people crazy, or cause disease and death, the effect of others is good, soothing and beneficial.'

Other historical figures who have commented on this include Michel Nostradamus (1503–1566). He wrote: 'Where plants perish and animals are absent, there you should not live, the place is unhealthy. You will experience disharmony and lose your poise. When you, however, find the place where happy, vital and healthy people live, and many old folk are in good health, then stay there, you will soon do without medicine or physician. The mysterious forces of the Earth will make you healthy.'

Geopathic stress does not only affect human beings. If it did, we might wonder if it were only an imaginary phenomenon. The effects of chi-paths and of the background etheric energy field also extends to plants and animals. Much can be learned about the energetic qualities and anatomy of a place by looking at the growth and health of its plants and the movement and sleeping or nesting patterns of both wild and domestic animals.

Some plants and animals are lovers of yin chi. These include many of the medicinal herbs, mushrooms, members of the nightshade family and ivy. Insects and burrowing animals are generally yin chi lovers, and cats tend to seek out and spend long periods on yin chi spots.

By contrast, other plants and animals do not tolerate strong, unbalanced yin chi and prefer more yang in their immediate environment. These include fruiting trees, beech trees, roses and geraniums, and vegetables that come to a head above ground. Birds, horses and dogs are also in this category, along with human beings.

If we allow ourselves, we can all pick up on the feel of a place in a broad and general way. Using dowsing, however, we can learn to read and interpret the particular characteristics of chi polarity, intensity and flow in a very focused and specific way, thereby refining and enhancing the quality and health of our relationship with our environment, on both a large and small scale.

Dowsing the earth's energies

We can use our pendulum for much of our dowsing in relation to earth energies, but it is also useful to use another of the basic dowsing tools.

Dowsing with the L-rod

This dowsing tool, so-called because of its shape, can be constructed from any material. It can be easily made at home by cutting and bending a metal coat hanger into the necessary shape. You will need a pair of rods, one for each hand. Mostly used for searching for things while the dowser moves around, L-rods can also be used for 'Yes/No' questions in a sitting or standing position.

Find a comfortable posture, with the spine erect and shoulders relaxed. Hold the shorter part of the rod firmly but gently, near to vertical, without touching the longer, horizontal part of the rod. Your forearms should be approximately horizontal, your elbows bent at around 90°. Your hands should be comfortable, probably about 30cm/1ft apart.

Practice your 'Yes' and 'No' movements until they seem easy and familiar. To find your 'Yes, but...', go all the way over for your 'Yes' signal, and

L-ROD RESPONSES
These show a range of L-rod responses

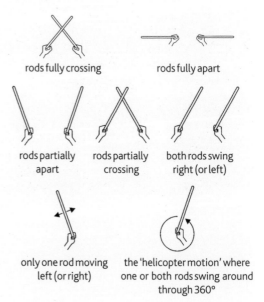

rods fully crossing

rods fully apart

rods partially apart

rods partially crossing

both rods swing right (or left)

only one rod moving left (or right)

the 'helicopter motion' where one or both rods swing around through 360°

ESTABLISHING 'YES' AND 'NO' RESPONSES
The two basic L-rod responses are rods-splitting-apart and rods-closing-together. See what you get when you try to establish your 'Yes/No' responses in the preparation stages for L-rod dowsing.

1 Hold the rods pointing straight out and away from you, parallel with each other. This is the neutral, or search position.

2 Keeping the rods the same distance apart, move them to the dominant side of your body. As you do this, ask 'Please show me my response for Yes'. See what the rods give for a signal.

3 Having done that, go back to your middle, neutral position, and then go over to the opposite side stating 'Please show me my response for No', and observe what this response will be.

then come a third of the way back towards neutral, asking for the signal. Repeat this process to find your 'No, but...'. Lastly, with your rods in neutral, ask for your 'Unanswerable question' response. As with the pendulum, if you do not get automatic responses, you can programme pre-determined movements for your rods.

Searching for dragons

Now that we are familiar with L-rods, we will use them to discover dragons in the landscape.

To begin you will need to be centred and grounded. Clear your mind, and visualize yourself in a column of golden light. Standing comfortably with your rods in their neutral position, state: 'I wish to dowse for earth energies', then ask: 'Is this timely and appropriate?' If the response is 'Yes', then proceed: 'Please show me any energy paths of significance to my health.' Now walk forwards at a slow but steady pace.

When you reach the first path, your rods will start to split apart as though meeting something solid like a wall. Once they are completely apart, you have arrived at an energy line. This is your 'Here it is!' signal. (You may find instead that the rods cross, this is also a 'Here it is!' signal.)

Although this response may be the same as that for your 'Yes' or 'No', in this context it is simply showing you the location of the dragon as requested. Each energy path will have two edges and a middle. Sometimes, the larger ones appear to have several edges on each side, somewhat similar to the layers of the human subtle body, lacking only the final, physical layer.

Step back until your rods are in neutral position and then, ask 'Please show me the nearest edge of this energy line', and dowse forwards until you find it. Step back and return to neutral once again and then ask to be shown the furthest edge of the line, dowsing forwards until you find that. Some lines are very narrow, while others are several metres or feet across. Having defined the edges of the line, you can also dowse for the centre of the path.

Next, ask 'Is this a yin chi-path?' 'Yes' or 'No' will tell you its polarity, and then ask 'More than...?' and 'Less than...?' questions to establish its strength on a scale of 1 to 10. Finally, dowse for the direction of flow, and the path that it takes through the space. To track the energy, either step sideways dowsing into the edge or centre repeatedly until you have traced out the extent of the path, or use the directional dowsing technique.

DIRECTIONAL DOWSING

This method is primarily used for tracking the path of dragons, places where they cross or for finding lost items, whether it is a ring, the way out of a wood or to a particular place. It is a very simple technique.

1 Stand in the centre of the dragon holding one rod out at arm's length, pointing away from you. (If you are looking for a direction to a place, it does not matter where you stand.)

2 Slowly turn your body through 360° asking 'Please show me the direction in which the dragon flows (or lost object can be found).' The rod will seem to stick in one direction.

3 Turn to face this direction, place your L-rods in the search position and ask 'Please show me when I arrive.' Walk forwards in that direction until you get your 'Here it is!' response.

Dragons and auras

▲ The dragon is the symbol of energy in motion, whether it represents the body of the earth or the body of a person.

One of the ways that we can understand and assess the effect that different chi-paths have upon us is to observe the changes in one of the layers of the human subtle body, known as the health aura. This layer is a sphere around us, typically found between 45cm/18in to 1m/3ft out from our physical body. It can be observed to expand and contract in a dynamic and flexible manner depending on our current level of personal vitality and the presence or absence of any stressful or beneficial influences upon us.

Dowsing for auras

To dowse for the subtle body or health aura, you will need two people, one to dowse, and one to be the subject of the exercise.

To begin, both people need to get clear and centred, and visualize themselves in golden light.

Next, place your L-rods in search position and state: 'I wish to dowse for changes in the health aura of (name)'. Ask: 'Is this timely and appropriate?'

If 'Yes', first have your subject stand in a neutral spot, that is somewhere where you can't find any dragons. Stand about 3m/10ft away from your subject, facing them. With your L-rods in search position, state clearly 'Please show me the edge of (name's) health aura'.

Walk towards them until your rods swing apart. This is the current position of their health aura. You may be able to feel it with your hands, a very subtle sensation like feeling the edge of a soap bubble.

Dowsing on a dragon

Now, stand your subject on the edge of a yin chi-path, positioned at a right-angle to the energy flow. They should be facing away from the centre of the path, with its edge running under the middle of their feet.

Have them stand there for about a minute, noticing any sensations in their body, or changes in mood.

Now, re-dowse their health aura. You are likely to find that it has contracted towards their body. Following this, stand them on the centre of the path, again at a right angle to the flow, the energy moving either left to right or right to left around them. Have them stand on the centre of the path for about a minute, noticing any sensations in their body, or changes in mood.

Re-dowse their health aura again. This time, you are likely to find that the subtle body has expanded outwards.

Repeat this exercise with a yang chi-path. Again ask your subject to notice their feelings, moods and any sensation they may have in their body. Then observe the effects on the health aura, both at the centre and at the edges of the path.

Finding intersections

Where dragons meet, their energies merge and enhance each other, creating and intensifying the etheric field and magnifying their effects.

There are very many tiny chi-paths all over the surface of the earth, almost like the lines that go to make up our fingerprints, or the web a spider weaves. This is the earth's capillary network, an etheric web or matrix, distributing chi in an even, gentle manner to every point on the surface of the planet. Most of these lines are so tiny that they do not have a directly significant effect on our health. Only the larger chi-paths and lines of the energetic web will cause immediate changes in our health aura, and these are the dragons that we are concerned with. If you dowse simply for any chi-paths or lines of dowseable energy you will find very many tiny lines. This is why we should qualify when we dowse, and ask to be shown chi-paths of significance to our health when looking for dragon intersections.

To find a chi-path intersection, use the L-rod directional dowsing technique. As you are following the flow of the chi with pointed L-rods, ask your dowsing to show you a chi-path intersection. Walk forwards until you get a 'Here it is!' response.

Assessing crossing dragons

Having found the chi-path intersection, identify the edges and middle of each path, and the polarity, strength and direction of flow. Using your ten-point scale (use 'More than...?' and 'Less than...?' questions with your 'Yes' and 'No'

dowsing), you can also find the individual and combined strength of the two lines. (You may need to go above ten on your scale for combined strength, as the effect of crossing paths is often multiplicative rather than additive.)

Place your subject on these intersection points and dowse the effects on their health aura. Yin-yin intersections often reduce the health aura to a very tight, contracted area close in around the physical body; yang-yang intersections move the health aura further out than usual.

Where the yin and yang paths meet we find the greatest expansion of all, sometimes pushing the health aura out by several metres or yards. This is a consequence of the synergistic, creative energy available when the opposite qualities combine. These synergistic points are known as power-centres.

Clearing and grounding

Chi-paths can have dramatic effects on us, and at the end of this exercise we need to clean, clear and ground ourselves.

First find a neutral spot and visualize and affirm that you are clean, clear, full of golden light, perfectly healthy and whole.

When you have finished, dowse to ensure that your subject's health aura is returned to its original size or larger – if it is diminished use one of the healing techniques that we learned earlier to restore and balance their energy.

YIN/YANG INTERSECTION
Where yin chi-paths and yang chi-paths cross the energy field is intensified.

yang chi-path (fire dragon)
straight energy path

yin chi-path (water dragon) vein of underground water

yin/yang intersection

Geopathic stress

Geopathic stress is best considered as a dysfunction in the relationship between person and place. It has two basic causes.

The first cause of geopathic stress is when we spend extended periods of time in etheric energy fields which, by their nature, are simply not conducive to human health. The majority of these cases are of people exposed to strong yin chi-paths which, being of a relatively more receptive nature than the human etheric body, absorb, drain and deplete our subtle energies. At a mental level this causes fatigue, poor concentration, impaired communication and diminished tolerance for challenge and stress. At an emotional level the effects are feeling low and introverted, and at a physical level, of immune system depletion. Very often, biological cycles are also disturbed.

Ideally, building sites are dowsed before construction begins to ensure a healthy environment

▼ Use L-rods to dowse inside buildings to check for the presence of geopathic stress. If possible, dowse a plot of land before you buy it to assess whether it is compatible with human health or not.

for humans. If a building has been constructed on imbalanced or yin chi-paths, it will not be healthy unless the basic nature of the energy present can be repatterned.

The second cause of geopathic stress is when an otherwise benevolent and healthy energy field becomes stressed and traumatized, and the chi-flow is disturbed, blocked or imbalanced. This is typically the result of traumatic changes to the landscape such as quarrying, excavation, or new construction projects. The effects on us are similar to being exposed to strong yin chi-paths. In this case however, healing needs to be applied to restore balance to an otherwise healthy place.

Assessing and working with geopathic stress

It is possible to enter a creative dialogue with the spirit of place. If timely and appropriate, and supported by the place, our strongly held and clearly focused thoughts can influence and repattern the etheric field. This allows both for healing and repatterning of the basic nature of the earth's subtle body to occur in a gentle and respectful way.

Let us for example assume that we are assessing a small space – perhaps a room that we have as our main living area – where we will spend extended time on a daily basis. Before dowsing, clear and centre yourself, and visualize yourself in a column of golden light connecting you with the source of love and healing, and check your 'Yes' signal: 'I want to find out about the energy in this room. Is this timely and appropriate?' If 'Yes', then ask: 'Are there any energies in this room that are detrimental to human health?' If so, find out if they are detrimental because of their nature, or because of a trauma of some kind.

If the chi has been traumatized, there is likely one or more blocked or overly stimulated chi-paths running through the space. Let your dowsing guide you to where to work, using your L-rods or pendulum, much as you would when directing healing towards a person. It can seem strange to speak with something that we cannot see, but let yourself engage with love with the spirit of place.

REPATTERNING ENERGY

If you find a chi-path in your space that is, by its nature, detrimental to your health, you will need to ask the spirit of place that the energy be redistributed. Remember that the energy itself is neither good nor bad, and that something that may be harmful to us, can be helpful to other species; if we approach energy that is detrimental to humans as something undesirable we might logically think we should try to eradicate it, but this can have very damaging consequences. When you are ready to start, visualize yourself channelling healing energy from the source of love and healing, and ask that the etheric field receive whatever healing energy that it needs to regain a state of health and balance, peace and vitality.

1 Hold your pendulum and begin dialogue by saying: 'I wish to dialogue with the spirit of place here. Is this timely and appropriate?' If the answer is 'Yes', continue by stating: 'I wish to spend time in this space and need the energy here to be supportive to my health.' Ask: 'Are you willing to repattern the energy here to be supportive of my health?' If 'Yes', ask: 'Are you able to repattern the energy here to be supportive of my health?' If it is, it may be able to do this itself or it may require your loving energy to help it to do so.

3 Once your dowsing indicates that the repatterning has occurred, give thanks to the spirit of place, ask a blessing for the place, and end the healing sequence as you have before.

Sometimes the repatterning may take hours or days. Check with your dowsing to see if it needs further help. Once it is complete, dowse the space again to assess the location and nature of the energies present.

If the spirit of place will support you, you will experience immense personal benefit from living in an entirely healthy space.

2 If the spirit of place is both willing and able, make a special request, almost like a prayer:

'I request that the energy in this space be repatterned at this time to be supportive of human health at every level, and that it may remain so for as long as may be the divine will.'

This request focuses your intention in a respectful and responsible way that will initiate the changes that you need. If the spirit of place is willing but is not able to repattern the energy field for you, ask if it can do so with your help.

Space clearing

Geopathic stress affects us primarily at an etheric level, the layer of energy nearest to the physical. Problems can also occur, however, in other layers of the earth's subtle body, particularly the emotional and mental levels of energy and consciousness. This follows our understanding of the body-mind-spirit connection, and of the intricate correlation between the energetic anatomy of all things, whether person, plant or planet.

Most often when a place or area becomes traumatized at the level of emotion or thought, it is as a direct consequence of intense and emotionally traumatic human activity. The most classic example of this is on previous battlegrounds. Often when we visit such sites, we are aware of the intense effect they have upon us, powerfully impacting our mood and our thoughts, often for days, even weeks after our visit. The atmosphere at these places is almost tangible.

It is not healthy for a place to hold such memories. In health, energy is free to move and flow. Emotional and mental trauma creates frozen, dis-

▼ Space clearing cleanses and re-integrates the emotional energy in a place; a powerful and important healing process.

▲ There are many tools and techniques which can be used to focus our intent in space clearing, including sound cymbals. Use whatever feels most natural to you and appropriate for the space.

integrated pockets of energy in space and time. Having learned to work with chi-paths and the etheric layer, we need next to learn how to bring peace and healing into the related layers of emotion and thought.

Clearing negative place memory

Healing at this level is becoming known as space clearing. When working to bring a place into a state of peace and balance, the chi-paths and other patterns of the etheric layer should generally be addressed first. If they are not addressed, the space clearing is unlikely to be fully effective.

As with our previous healing work, be guided by your dowsing. The clearing, centring, and visualization of golden light before and after these exercises is very important. It is easy to resonate with energetic problems and disturb our own subtle body when dowsing or healing a person. It is even easier for this to occur when working with disturbances in place, because the energy field of place has so much more psychic mass and presence than that of a person. Be disciplined about cleaning and clearing before and after you work, and ask that you may also be healed through the process. If you find after a healing process, either with a person or a place, that you are feeling ill at ease or out of sorts, take time for personal healing and cleansing or, better still, ask someone else with healing and dowsing skills to do this for you. It is good for healers and dowsers to support each other in this way.

Whichever method we decide to try, the most important part of space clearing is our intention for it to occur. Use any tools that feel comfortable to you in a simple and authentic way. It can be powerful to use combinations, particularly if all four elements are represented.

▶ Dowsing will help you to assess the need for space clearing and will guide your healing process.

USING THE ELEMENTS
Space clearing can be achieved in many ways. All of them share the common intent that any trauma held in the place be gently released and the energy dissolved and re-integrated into the system in a harmless and healthy form. We can enhance and focus our intention for this to happen using any tools or techniques that feel authentic and helpful. Traditionally, these are considered within the elements of earth, water, air and fire.

Earth
• Salt is a classic cleanser of energy. You can leave salt in a room in a dish overnight or for a few days and then dispose of it outside to remove detrimental energy and return it to the earth.
• Eggs are also effective space clearers. Leave one overnight in a traumatized room and the egg will absorb any detrimental energy present. Dispose of the egg outdoors for the earth to recycle.

Water
• Water from holy wells carries naturally healing energy. You can also bless water yourself by channelling healing energy into it.

• Adding salt to water improves its clearing properties, and adding flower essences is extremely effective for healing the place memory.
• Sprinkle the water around, pour it on the ground, or spray it into the air through an atomizer.

Air
• Burning incense (powder or sticks), aromatic oils or cleansing herbs releases their healing energies into the space.
• Sage, cedar, lavender and rue are all good cleansers. You can burn them in a dish and send the smoke into all parts of the space with your hand or with a fan or feather. In the native American tradition, the use of sage in this way is often called smudging.
• Healing and cleansing sounds such as chanting, singing, bell ringing and rattling, also come under the element of air and can be used in space clearing rituals.

Fire
• Whether the fire of an individual candle flame or a large bonfire lit outdoors, fire is a powerful cleanser and transformer of energy.

Landscape Synergy

'...some places differ from one another in their tendency to breed better and worse human beings... of all these places, those territories which would differ the most would be those that have some divine presence in the winds and are under the care of demons, and hence receive those who come to settle each time either graciously or in the opposite way.'

PLATO (C. 427 – 347BCE)

Living with the spirit of place

We have been introduced to the concept of the spirit of place, and considered the subtle energy anatomy of the earth and the nature of the etheric, emotional and mental levels of the subtle body. We can now dowse to find and assess chi-paths, work with healing to restore balance within these fields, and endeavour to create a healthy environment for ourselves. It remains now to weave these threads together and place them in the context of everyday life.

The reason that we are unfamiliar with many of these concepts and lacking even a common language to discuss them is because of the extraordinary personal power that this awareness brings to us. Knowing where the centres of etheric energy are in the environment gives one the ability both to influence the consciousness and the spirit of the landscape and to draw on its power for personal use. They are nodal points on the earth's energetic web, open channels for the bilateral exchange of energy and information.

Any intention that we bring to such places, will be greatly charged and energized. In recent times,

▲ Everywhere, whatever the location, has its own special spirit of place. Tutelary spirits vary widely in character, and may correspond to the landscape in which they choose to reside. Ask yourself why you are here now, and what is here for you to learn?

an understanding of their nature has been almost entirely lost or forgotten. The return to holism leads us back to the spirit of the land however, and now we can learn about, gain access to and interact with the intensified energies of power-centres and enter conscious dialogue with the spirit of these places.

The sacred relationship

In modern times, we have grown increasingly fearful for the safety and well-being of our spirit here on earth. Far from its being our hostile enemy, we are in a sacred relationship with the spirit of the landscape, which has nurtured us and holds a place for us within it. Generously and selflessly it offers us everything that we need, not only physically but also emotionally, mentally and spiritually.

We can regain this sacred relationship simply by changing our attitude to one of love, respect and engagement.

The human spirit has been on a long journey through the darkness of separation and introspection in order to know itself. Now it is time to look outside ourselves and to reconnect in sacred relationship with all the other members of the universal family.

Tutelary spirits

One of the gifts offered to us by the spirit of the landscape is to tutor us in relationship both with ourselves and with all that is outside us. For this reason, the spirit of place has often been known as the tutelary spirit. Each place in the landscape holds a particular consciousness for us to engage with and experience, and has lessons, challenges and teaching experiences to offer us.

Most of us are familiar with the way that phases of our life are associated with periods of time spent in a given location. We mostly think of these periods in terms of the activities that we were engaged with during that time, whether growing up, going to school, college, having our first job and so on. But the changes that each move brings are much deeper than simply the outward changes. We learn and grow in a place until we have received what it has to offer us – the teachings our spirit needs on its journey – and then we move on, naturally, to the next teacher, the next tutelary spirit.

This process of growth and learning can be greatly eased and made more joyful if we engage with it in a conscious and celebratory way rather than ignoring it or resisting all change as being fearful and painful.

The power of imagination

To receive help, tutoring and guidance from the world of spirit, all that we need do is to ask for it. Tutelary and other spirits may not interfere with human free will, but perhaps a good use of our free will is to ask respectfully for help and support in meeting life's many and perplexing challenges.

Having asked for guidance, we need then to pay very close attention to the information that we receive in return. This can come to us

in many ways: as synchronous events, as unexpected change, as things that we read, as dreams and ideas, even as work or people we meet. Spirit moves in mysterious ways. The most powerful tool that we have in our psyche for dialogue with the spirit world is our imagination. We have long been led to distrust and discard this precious part of ourselves. To reclaim the power of our direct, personal connection with spirit we need to reclaim the power of our exciting and imaginal reality.

Through dreams, images and inspiration of every tone and colour, our imagination is the creative canvas for us to receive ideas and understanding from the unseen worlds, and upon which we can visualize, create and project our own energies and intentions out into the world.

In this way we are invited to expand our awareness and take a role of responsibility and leadership in our life. Whoever we are, wherever we may be, we are in sacred relationship with the tutelary spirits of time and place that we have, however unconsciously, been attracted and drawn to in order to support us through the journey of life. Open your imagination and your consciousness to engage with them in dialogue. Pay close attention…

▼ It is important to spend time within a landscape and appreciate it for its uniqueness.

The spirit of a home

Our home is the place with which we establish a primary bond of intimacy and identity, and because we spend so much time, and allow ourselves to be so open and vulnerable there, the state and nature of its subtle energetic environment is a core factor in determining our overall health.

Dowsing your home

The practice of dowsing will help to deepen your awareness of the nature and character of your home, and orient you to high and low energy spots and the flow of chi through it. It also gives you a means of dialogue with the spirit of place.

You can use either your pendulum or L-rods for the opening dialogue of 'Yes' and 'No' questions and answers, and your L-rods for identifying and tracking the energy paths through your home.

Clear and centre yourself, and visualize yourself in a column of golden light. Introduce yourself

▼ Rooms that work well in a house tend to have a good match of their energy to their function. Rooms where the energy field is incongruous to the use of space feel awkward and difficult.

first. State the nature of your relationship with the place, and your intentions, whether it is a home or also your work place, and so forth. For instance: 'I am (name) and this is my home. I live here with my family and wish this to be a safe and nurturing place to live. I wish to communicate with the spirit of place here. Is this timely and appropriate?'

If the answer is 'Yes' then go on. 'Is this a safe and healthy place for me to live? Is there anything that I need to know about the energy here? Is any healing required in this space? Are there any chi-paths of health significance that run through this space? Are there any power-centres here?'

Gather as much information as you can, dowsing with 'Yes/No' questions. Once you have an overall feel for the energy field, dowse room by room to find out the peace or otherwise of the energies present, whether any healing is needed, and what the overall polarity and field intensity is using a ten-point scale.

Chi-paths in your space

Get to know the energetic anatomy of your space as intimately as you can. If there are any chi-paths

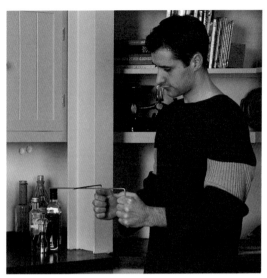

▲ The most important place to have healthy and gentle energy is in our bed, especially for children. Do you sleep well? Do you wake feeling refreshed?

▲ Becoming intimate with the spirit of your home will deepen your relationship with the space. Keep high-use areas energetically clear and well balanced.

present, find them with your L-rods and track them through the room, then on through the house and outside – you will want to track these all the way from where they enter your property to where they leave. Find out their polarity and intensity, their state of peace or trauma, and how they affect the human health aura.

Notice the health of any plants that you find on the chi path, and whether it runs under beds or chairs or through places where animals sleep. It is best not to spend prolonged periods sitting or standing directly in chi-paths, particularly if they are of a strong yin nature.

Energy fields to activities

Different energy fields are appropriate for different human activities. During sleep for example, it is most appropriate to be in a serene, very gentle and moderate energy field, without any strong or highly polarized chi. Ideally our bed is placed where only the tiny capillary lines of chi feed a constant and gentle energy to us. The bed and bedroom generally should be kept in a state of energetic clarity and cleanliness. Healing any etheric traumas and clearing the space of disturbed

memory is important before you start using a bedroom. You may also want to clear and balance the energy after an argument or any period of illness, or if your dreams seem troubled and tense. If you routinely sleep heavily and wake unrefreshed you should dowse carefully to ensure that there is not an excess of yin chi running through your bed.

If you do find energetic problems in your bedroom, apply the healing techniques that we have learned. Ask for the help and co-operation of the spirit of place to ease and repattern the energy flow and create a safe and nurturing space for you.

You may find one or more power spots in your home ; these are ideal areas for any creative activity, whether cooking, writing, painting, doing healing work or other spiritual practices. It is best to limit your time in intense power-centres and it is very important to keep them clean and clear, because they hold and amplify thoughts and emotions.

Cleaning and clearing a space can be as simple as asking the spirit of place to heal and balance all the energies there, or you may need to use one or more tools such as bells, candles, incense and so on to raise enough focused intention to restore health. Your dowsing will guide you.

The spirit of work

The energy fields most suitable for work depend on the nature of the work itself. The standard Chinese formula for human activity space is for there to be a relationship between yang and yin chi, in a 3:2 ratio respectively. This gives us exposure to both polarities but gives us a slightly expansive energy overall. However, some tasks are best performed in a very serene environment, and others require a higher level of intense energy.

As with our relationship with the landscape, it is time for us to reclaim the sacred nature of work in our lives. Dowsing for geopathic stress in the workplace is important as it can have effects on the dynamics between members of staff, and the success of the business itself.

When assessing work space, first meet and greet the spirit of place. Next dowse generally to discover the nature, quality and health of the energy field overall, and then dowse further, area by area, to become intimately familiar with the energetic anatomy of the etheric field.

Ideally, match the functional use of the space to the energy field present or, if this is not possible,

▼ When the energy field of a place is balanced and harmonious, creative work tends to go smoothly.

ask the spirit of place that the field be repatterned to support your activities there. Perform any healing or clearing for the space as necessary.

Geopathic stress at work

One very important consideration for a business is to ascertain whether the overall energy field of the business premises are well matched to the basic nature of the business, that is, whether the spirit of your enterprise is compatible with the spirit of that place. If your business is three-years-old or more and is thriving in its current location, then the answer to this question is almost certainly 'Yes'. If it is less than three years old or is not thriving, then your dowsing may hold the key to the long-term success or failure of your enterprise.

Business premises that are geopathically stressed or that carry significantly traumatized place memory will often have a rapid turnover of business occupants. A new business will move in, fail to thrive, and either fail altogether or soon move out. The next business is likely to have a similar fate.

One of the core understandings and observations of working with the energy field of place is that any given place, in the absence of focused energetic intervention, will exhibit a repeating pattern in the lives and health of sequential occupants or residents. This applies to all places, whether commercial, public or domestic.

In a business environment, signs that there is geopathic stress or traumatic place memory include a high sickness rate, poor communication between employees and management, poor concentration, low creativity, low productivity, lethargy and depression. Members of the public may intuitively avoid coming into a stressed retail space, and there are often problems with goods assembled in a stressed manufacturing location. Geopathic stress in an office space has a direct impact on the performance and health of those working there.

Planting a business in an energy field is similar to planting a flower in the garden. To thrive it will need the right kind of nurturing conditions. If you are looking for new business premises, either to

▲ The locations where we spend the most time are the most important to check and balance carefully.

start a new business or to expand an existing one, take your pendulum and L-rods with you when you go to look at the prospective site.

Greet the spirit of place there and let it know who you are and what your business intentions are. Ask if this is a location where your business would be welcome and nurtured and would thrive. Phrase your questions carefully and pay close attention to the answers. A straight 'No' should send you looking elsewhere. A 'Yes, but...' or a 'No, but...' answer may suggest that healing or repatterning is required or that the location might offer itself for something different than you had originally intended. Allow the spirit of place to offer you its insight and inspiration. Check any ideas that you might get with your dowsing.

Of course a straight 'Yes' speaks for itself. If you have several locations to choose from, you can ask: 'Is this the best location for my business?'. Time spent dowsing before committing to new projects is time well invested.

Matching tasks to locations

In an established work location, where the spirit is supportive and the energy fields balanced, harmonious and clean, the main consideration is of matching tasks to relevant locations.

Tasks that involve long periods in one place, that require sustained focus or attention to detail or that involve operating dangerous machinery should be performed where the energy field is very serene, well-balanced and even. One does not want strongly polarized or locally intense chi or chi-paths in such places or for such tasks.

Tasks that require relatively short, unsustained bursts of creativity or inspiration will be well supported by yang chi-paths and power-centres.

Yin-chi locations should be avoided other than for brief periods of introspection and grounding or for letting go of intense emotional energy. Equipment is more likely to fail or give trouble if it is in a yin-chi location.

Finally, consider making major decisions on the largest power-centre available, assuming that it is clean and harmonious. This is the location where you can receive the most clear guidance and support from the tutelary spirit, where your intuition will be most powerfully engaged and where your intentions will carry their best energy.

▼ For a human to be fully healthy, their work must be a loving and joyful act of self-expression, no matter how simple. Work becomes more creative and fun this way and less of a routine chore.

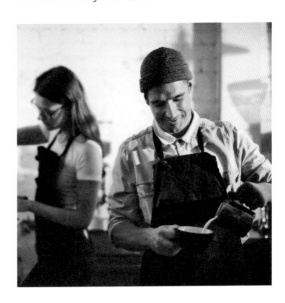

Dowsing in the garden

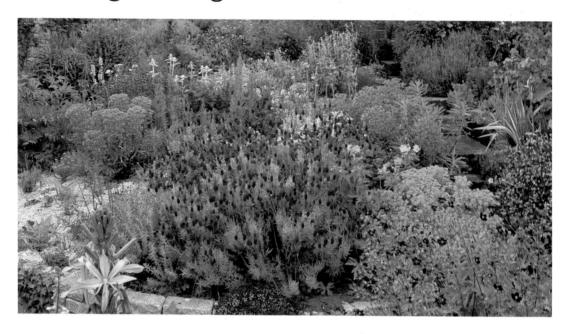

Dowsing is of immense use in the garden. It allows us to communicate with the spirit of place. We can trace chi-paths through the garden and identify any power-centres present, allowing us to organize the planting in synergy with a natural pattern. Dowsing helps us select the most appropriate plants for a location.

Devic and elemental spirits

The overall growth and vitality of plant life is the domain of nature spirits called devas. These spirits will help and guide us in our relationship with plants and will act both as our gardening allies and tutors. Using the power of your imagination, you can dialogue with the devic spirits in your garden.

Centre and clear yourself, and visualize yourself in a column of golden light. Check your 'Yes' signal. Introduce yourself and state your intentions: 'I am (name) and this is my garden. I would like to grow beautiful flowers here and also fruit and vegetables to feed my family. I wish to communicate with the principal deva of this garden. Is this timely and appropriate?' Next ask if you are in the appropriate location for communication; it may be

▲ Laying out a garden with reference to the spirit of place, and to the underlying pattern of subtle energies, greatly enhances its health and beauty.

that it doesn't matter where in the garden you are, however if this does matter, use an L-rod in an outstretched arm and slowly turn your body around in a circle while asking: 'Show me the direction to go to communicate with the principal deva here.'

When the rod sticks are in one direction, walk that way with both of your L-rods in search position, asking for the exact spot until your get your 'Here it is!' response.

Let yourself become still and quiet, and then openly share with the deva all your thoughts about the garden. Through a process of dialogue, using the power of your imagination and by checking specific points with 'Yes/No' dowsing, see if you can find a co-creative strategy for planting and managing the space in collaboration with the devic spirit. Once you have an overall plan, you may wish to 'take a walk with the deva' and go around the garden, dowsing different areas to see if your ideas are at their best or could be improved.

Soils, seeds and seedlings

Dowsing is a valuable tool in helping us assess the overall necessity and specific requirements for soil amendments in our garden in a particular spot or even for an individual plant. This can be done by dowsing at the spot, or else back in the kitchen with a soil sample, or even over a gardening catalogue. 'Does the rose bed in the west corner need manure this season? Does it need any phosphate? Would this brand be best? Or this brand?'

You can also dowse to pick seeds out of a catalogue using your dowsing. 'Would this kind of tomato do well here? Would this kind do better?' You can also dowse over the seed-packets to find the exact spot to plant them in.

If you have brought a new plant into your garden, it is likely to thrive best if planted somewhere that it likes. You can dowse for its best location, for any soil amendments that it needs, even for its orientation. 'Round to the right a little further? Further still?' You can use your dowsing to help you keep an eye on it while it re-establishes itself in its new location. 'Is it getting enough water?

▼ Dowsing allows a creative dialogue with your garden and a personal interaction with its spirit.

PLANT CHI PREFERENCES
Use this list as a starting point for discovering the chi preferences for different species. You can then dowse plants from your own garden to find out their preferences, and compile your own gardening list.

Yin chi-lovers
beans, larch, medicinal herbs, oak, sycamore, tomatoes, ivy

Yin chi-avoiders
beech, Brussels sprouts, cauliflower, cucumber, elm, fruit trees, lime, peas

Too much?' This can be helpful with species that are difficult to grow or that are at the edge of their climate tolerance, or that have not arrived in your garden in the best of health.

Chi-paths and power-centres

As with your home and work space, find out as much as you can about the etheric, emotional and mental energy fields of your garden. Perform any necessary healing and clearing work, and ask the deva whether etheric repatterning would be helpful and appropriate to support the garden overall. Not only will plants grow better when the energies are clean, clear, balanced and harmonious, but you will also attract many more birds and other wildlife into your garden if the energy is sweet. It will make the garden much more friendly for you, and greatly increase the vitality of any food grown.

Finally, bear in mind that different species have different preferences and consider the pattern of chi-paths and the chi preferences for each. There is a starter list above, but you will learn most by dowsing and observing your own garden. Plants grown where they are not supported by the available chi will be weak and stunted, prone to disease and frost, and generally less healthy. Everything that lives in your compost heap and helps create it would love to be overcrossing yin chi-paths, and bees also like to live overcrossing yin chi-paths, so place their hives there if you can.

Energy and power-centres

A power-centre is a point in the earth's etheric web where yin and yang chi are both present. The effect of bringing these polar-opposite, elemental forces together is to create a synergistic union where the energetic outcome is greater than that which either the yin or the yang energy can achieve on its own. It is the same energetic fusion that allows the creation of new life through sexual union.

To place ourselves in the energy field of these nodal points is to put ourselves in a profoundly creative space. There are many consequences of this. One of these is that a very deep form of healing and renewal becomes available to us. Because the full spectrum of yin and yang energy is present, we can draw on any part of that spectrum to replenish stressed and depleted parts of our own energy field. Also, our subtle body is exposed to a larger, more powerful energy field that is whole and irrepressibly creative, and we can draw on this potential energy to heal and recreate any parts of ourselves that have become damaged.

Power-centres are also the points in the landscape where the etheric, emotional and mental energies are most intensely present. This means that at these points qualities of spirit are more available to us, if we can open ourselves to them.

▲ Where elemental forces are strong and intense – even overpowering – mindfulness and clarity are essential for keeping us centred and balanced.

Health and balance
Owing to the intensity of their vibrational field, power-centres hold memory and information more than other parts of the energetic web, and their influence is greater upon us than when we are at other points on the web. It is therefore very important to keep power-centres clean and balanced.

Our relationship with them depends upon their size and intensity and how prepared we are to encounter them. We may enjoy the experience of paddling in lapping waves on a beach, or if we raise our energy, to match engaging the power of larger waves.

When we engage with power-centres, our own preparation and balance is therefore important. Whatever consciousness we hold when we enter a power-centre will be mirrored back to us and also projected into the surrounding energy field. If we are not in very good balance and enter a very large energy field, our own emotional or intellectual state may be magnified to a level that we find intensely uncomfortable.

POWER-CENTRE PRACTICE

• Let the power-centre become a place that you regularly visit, each time checking if it needs healing or balancing.

• Ask when you visit whether it is appropriate for you to be there at that particular time; sometimes it may need to be left to itself, and it might be better to return another day.

• Once you have identified the power-centre that you will be working with, take some time to greet the spirit there, and ask if it needs any healing, clearing or repatterning to come into its most whole and balanced state.

• Bring a spiritual practice, such as meditation, yoga or t'ai chi, to the power-centre. Even if you only visit and sit and use your imagination to open a dialogue with the spirit of the power-centre, you will find that your focus, clarity and energies improve.

• Communing regularly with a nodal point also powerfully attunes us with the rhythm and cycles of the earth, helping us to move with much more ease and fluidity through life.

• Visit your power-centre at sunrise, at noon, at sunset, at midnight, to get to know all of its moods, and in turn more about yourself.

Paradoxically, both healing and chaos can occur in power-centres. Which of these we will experience depends on the magnitude and balance of the power-centre itself and the balance of our own inner energies. However, it is also the case that healing and inspiration can come through chaos.

Locating your power-centre

As we become increasingly aware of subtle energy, it is appropriate to cultivate a relationship with a power-centre. Ideally, this occurs at two levels. The first level is to work with a power-centre in our own space. Whether large or small, there will be a yin/yang intersection in almost any place, and if there is not, you can call on the spirit of place to bring one. The second level at which to engage with power-centres is in the wider landscape where we can have access to larger energy fields.

Clear and centre yourself, visualize yourself in a column of golden light, and check your 'Yes' response. State: 'I wish to dowse about power-centres. Is this timely and appropriate?'

If 'Yes', ask: 'Is there a power-centre in this space that it would be good and healthy for me to be working with at this time?' If the answer is 'Yes', use your directional dowsing technique to guide you to its location. Typically it will be experienced as an enchanted place, and you may well know already where it is.

▼ Power-centres have immense capacity to inspire and transform. They offer themselves as spiritual doorways, and as nodal points for perceiving and influencing the wider landscape around them.

The geomantic landscape

Geomancy is the name given to the practice of reading and relating to the subtle energies of the earth. It is a core part of the relationship that all cultures have had with the environment and is intimately woven into the cultural fabric of indigenous people everywhere.

To both orientate themselves in their landscape and to connect in the most powerful and life-affirming way with the ever-changing, pulsing energies of spirit, all cultures have sought out and engaged in intimate relationships with power-centres. In the same way that communing with a power-centre in our garden connects us to the spirit of our home, the larger nodal points around us are places where the community can connect with the greater spirit of the land.

Power-centres are points of contact, and can function rather like umbilical cords, feeding and nourishing the spirit of an individual, of a com-

▼ Communities and cultures define themselves in reference to a particular place, rather like an umbilical point in their landscape. The path to it may often look like such a symbolic cord.

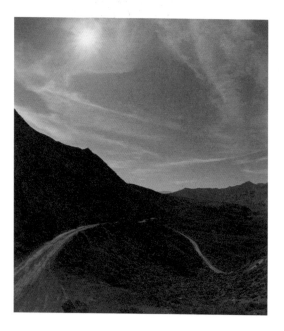

THE GEOMANCY ENERGIES
Magical cultures have referred to these awarenesses as the upper, middle and lower worlds. Human beings live in the middle world, influenced both by the dragon energies of the lower world and the planetary influences of the upper world. Or to put it another way, by the movement of energy in time and space.

• An awareness of the presence and influence of the dragon energies of the earth.

• An awareness of the presence and influence of the cyclical and celestial energies of the heavenly bodies.

• A recognition of the world of shape, pattern and form which is moved and guided by the two awarenesses above.

munity or even of an entire culture, depending on their magnitude. As we become allied with and are under the tutelage of the spirit of place in our home, so a nation becomes identified with and characterized by the spirit of the major power-centre that they claim as their point of reference, such as their capital city or most holy shrine.

Acts of pilgrimage

We not only need to develop an intimate relationship with our own personal power-centre, but to develop a relationship with the larger power-centres in the landscape occupied by our community.

Spending time in such places helps to attune us to the spirit of the wider landscape which holds, supports and meets the needs of our community. For the community to be healthy and sustaining, we all need to be in dialogue with the principal tutelary spirit of the landscape. This will guide us in how to form the right relationship with the seen and unseen forces that ultimately act to restore balance to all living systems.

▲ Simply being present is often all that is needed to receive the healing offered by a power-centre. Holy wells have a particularly sweet energy.

The act of pilgrimage has long been held as a spiritual journey to the holy places – the recognized power-centres – of the culture. Visiting these places was believed to offer a transformational journey of inspiration and healing at a deeply spiritual level. A return to the spiritual centre or focal point of the culture was to meet with its most powerful and enlightening spirits.

In many respects it does not matter what we do when we get there, it is simply the going and being present that is the key to the experience. To place our own subtle body in the intensified, healing, balancing and uplifting energy field of a major power-centre is enough.

Relationship with the land

Many power-centres are known and marked. You will find them in churches and cathedrals. You will find them in standing stones and stone circles, in medicine wheels, in kivas, in labyrinths, on sacred mountains and caves, and at holy wells, temples and shrines.

Some of them are not marked, however. The energies of the earth shift and repattern from time to time, and it is a while since the power-centres have been publicly explored and acknowledged in some places.

Issues of both environmental and personal health make healing our relationship with the spirit of the land vitally important at this stage in our evolution. We can do this in two ways. We need to engage in healing activities at power-centres, both old and new. This will help to clear them of the accumulated emotional, mental and psychic trauma that they have witnessed, and to help to ease, balance and restore the flow of chi in their dragons. The second way is by visiting them regularly, in a joyful and celebratory fashion, whether to sing, dance or meditate, to be healed, or spiritually transformed, or to have picnics and fly kites with our children. Simply we need to be there, and to steep ourselves in the wellspring of their nurturing, balancing, healing energy field.

Whichever route you take, don't forget to take your pendulum. Use it to find your spot where you can simply sit and be.

▼ Experiencing the subtle body of standing stones is a way to open us to the spirit of the landscape.

Dowsing Deeper

The hand moves
And the fire's whirling
Takes different shapes
All things change when we do –
The first word
'-Ah-'
Blossoms into all others
Each of them is true

KOOKAI, 5TH-CENTURY ZEN MASTER

Dowsing and water-witching

We have learned in this book to dowse with a focus on our health. This is one of the most powerful and useful applications for dowsing, and one in which, by our personal experience of its results, we can gain confidence in our abilities as dowsers, in the validity of dowsing as a technique, and of the power of following the wisdom of our spirit to guide us in our lives. While dowsing for health is of immense value, however, it is not its only use.

There is simply no limit to the potential uses of dowsing. We are limited only by our ability to ask clear, concise questions with 'Yes/No' answers, by our ability to remain engaged but unattached to the responses that we receive, and, apparently, by the authentic need for us to know the answer to the question that we have asked.

Water-witching

In many communities, dowsing (or divining as it is also called) is best known as a means of finding drinking water that can be reached by digging or drilling a well. In some places, water dowsers are known as water witches. Dowsing for water is an immensely valuable and practical application of

▲ To help you tune-in, you could imagine the water of a stream flowing around your hands.

the art. Competent water dowsers can identify not only the exact location of water in the earth, but also accurately predict its depth below the surface, its flow rate in quantity per minute or per hour, and its drinkable quality.

Dowsing for water is a natural ability that all humans have. The ability to find water in survival situations has embedded this capability deep in our psyche. When dowsing for water, as for anything else, we need to be as specific and focused as we can be with our questions. Let us assume that we are searching for water for a home:

First clear and centre yourself, and visualize yourself in a column of golden light. State: 'I want to dowse for water for this home'. Check your 'Yes' response. Then ask: 'Is this timely and appropriate?' If 'Yes', state: 'I need to find a source of good, pure, uncontaminated water, healthy for humans to drink, that will give a recoverable volume of 23 litres/5 gallons per minute, all year ' or whatever your requirements are.

Next ask: 'Is such a supply available on this piece of land?' You will need to predetermine where you may look (this will normally be dictated by property ownership).

If the answer to this question is 'No', continue dowsing until you discover what is available; perhaps there is a source of good water at 14 litres/3 gallons per minute, and you can accommodate your needs with this smaller volume by establishing a holding tank of a certain size. If the answer is 'Yes', you might then ask: 'Is there more than one source of such water?' If there is, you will want to determine which is the best source.

Considerations as to what constitutes the best source include the depth of the water (drilling further costs more and may require a more powerful pump), the volume available (if other houses are built nearby it will be good to have a productive well to share), the distance of the water from the house, and the drinkable quality (water is such a key part of our health and dietary needs that we might choose as a priority to drill for the very best, most health-giving water). There may also be local considerations of site practicality and access.

Identify which of the available sources best meets your needs with 'Yes/No' dowsing questions.

▼ L-rods are probably the most popular and widely used tools for water dowsing.

(You can also simply allow the wisdom of your spirit to guide you, asking to be shown the best source of water for a well, given all things known and unknown at this time.)

Dowsing for everything

Traditionally, and even now, dowsing is used for the location of minerals and oil. It has been applied in many military operations and has applications too useful to be dismissed as unconventional nonsense. Rescue teams as well as numerous police forces call on the services of dowsers to aid in search and recovery efforts. Construction crews routinely dowse to locate site utilities, and farmers dowse to find blocked or lost field drains.

You can dowse to see whether the cake is perfectly baked, whether the plant needs to be watered, whether one used car will be more reliable than another, whether the trouble is the carburettor or a spark plug, whether your client is genuinely creditworthy, whether the avocado will be ripe in time for Saturday dinner, even how many people will turn up at a party. The uses of dowsing are innumerable and only limited by your own imagination.

Let your dowsing be a friend. Treat it with respect, use it for reasonable and genuine need, and always check your answers with your common sense.

► Having clearly defined the quality and quantity of water that we need, we can begin dowsing to locate the whereabouts of a suitable source.

Further dowsing

Cultivating the dowser inside us is a process of gaining self-confidence and trust in the wisdom of our spirit, leading to a deep acceptance of our true self. It can become a vehicle for a powerful, self-led spiritual journey offering a personal channel for dialogue with the divine. Because of its power, for hundreds of years dowsing was outlawed by religious institutions who sought to control the spiritual direction of the community.

We now have the freedom to seek spiritually as we choose, but we should exercise caution if using dowsing purely as a tool for spiritual exploration and growth.

All dowsing falls broadly into two categories. The first is that of 'tangible target' dowsing, such as dowsing for missing objects, water, faults in car engines – things that have material substance and confirm our dowsing when we find them. The second category is 'intangible target' dowsing, such as dowsing for issues that can only be confirmed indirectly or subjectively. Spiritual dowsing falls into this category. We can sometimes become a little ungrounded and unbalanced if we only use our dowsing for intangible targets. Balance is the key.

▲ Dowsing offers a path of personal spiritual pilgrimage, safely guided by open heart and mind.

Locational dowsing

A further level of skill that we can develop is that of map dowsing; we treat the map as if it were the ground itself, as though we had a bird's eye view.

DOWSING ETHICS

There are many aspects to dowsing ethics, but these principles will support us in most situations.

• Dowsing is a personal tool. It gives you direct access to your spirit through your intuition. This helps you to both perceive and define reality – but only for yourself. You must be careful not to assume that because something is true for you that it is true for someone else.

• We all have our individual experience of spirit, which reveals itself to us in a form that we can each relate to. Please be careful not to impose beliefs that seem true to you upon others. Instead, share your discoveries and invite others to dowse for themselves. It's far healthier.

• Be careful not to engage in 'psychic trespass' through your dowsing. It is possible to use dowsing to discover things about other people and their concerns that they would prefer you did not know – private and confidential matters. To trespass in this way is thought to incur negative spiritual consequences, and in any case, it is not a respectful use of your dowsing.

• As a guiding rule, use your dowsing for those matters which are of genuine and reasonable concern to you personally or to others who have requested your help. Very occasionally, you may have to decide whether dowsing that appears to be in the overwhelming public interest justifies an intrusion upon another's privacy. Always dowse with integrity and you will not go far wrong.

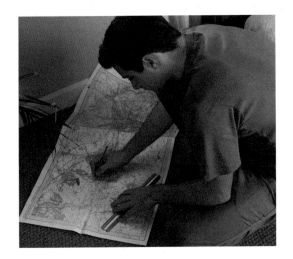

▲ Map dowsing can save a lot of time. Using a map allows you to dowse a large area quickly and with a large-scale map it can be surprisingly accurate.

If searching for a lost object or missing person, or for the best place to site a well, home or a sanctuary on a very large piece of land, or perhaps when tracing a dragon path across miles of open country, dowsing from a map is more practical than site dowsing in the first instance.

There are many techniques for map dowsing. The corner technique uses the pendulum to indicate a line of direction. Hold your pendulum over one corner of the map, swinging parallel with one edge. Ask for it to point towards the object of your search. Its swing will move round until it is swinging straight backwards and forwards, but now pointing in a direction that will lead you over the map. Follow this line with the pendulum itself or with a finger moving over the map until the pendulum changes its motion into your 'Yes' signal. This marks your spot. Confirm it by dowsing in from another corner for accuracy. If you are map-dowsing for a linear or sinuous feature such as a dragon path, ask your dowsing to indicate points along the path and then join up the dots.

The second technique is using a ruler. Let us assume we are looking for a single point – perhaps the location of a lost object that could be anywhere over a large area on a map. Prepare to dowse in the usual way, and when you are attuned and focused,

lay the map out flat and take a ruler or straight edge and lay it on the map at one side, and parallel with the edge. Start your pendulum swinging in neutral. Ask 'Please indicate when the ruler is at the location of the (name of object).' Move the ruler slowly over the map, keeping it parallel with one edge of the map. When your pendulum swings into its 'Yes' response, draw a pencil line down the ruler's edge. Now repeat this with the ruler parallel to the other edge of the map, at 90° to its previous orientation. Again, when your pendulum indicates that you have arrived at the spot, stop and draw a pencil line along the ruler's edge. Where the two lines cross is the spot that you are looking for.

In addition to direction finding on a map, there is also a site-dowsing technique for a pendulum, which is an adaptation of the L-rod method and is useful to know. Simply hold your pendulum in its neutral swing and ask it to show you in which direction the target is, point with your free hand or arm and slowly turn around until your pendulum swings into a 'Yes' response. Walk in that direction and ask it to indicate the point you need.

▼ With practice and experience, we can even dowse without tools, and use the natural sensitivity of our body to perceive intuitive information.

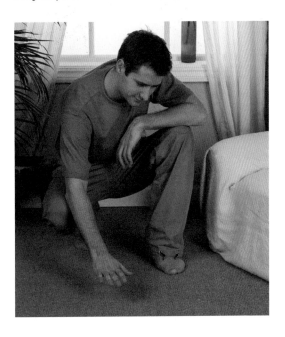

Fostering the inner healer

Some people have a gift for music. They are naturally inclined towards musicianship and may be exceptionally talented. Their gift can be channelled and focused and their abilities refined through learned skills and techniques. Even without training their ear for rhythm and melody and their passion for expressing themselves through music will bring pleasure both to themselves and to those around them. However, in the absence of self-consciousness, every single one of us can make a joyful noise and carry a tune to our own personal satisfaction, if not to the standard needed for a concert performance.

Healing gifts are similar to those for music. The gift of healing is held to be one of the gifts of the spirit, present in the very essence of who we truly are, and is not something learned or acquired. In the core of our being, we can all heal powerfully

▼ The small flame of an individual human spirit is of the same essence as the divine fire.

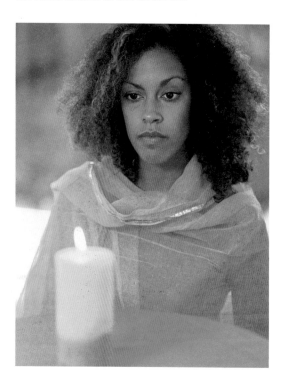

> Self-healing, and maintaining our personal centre and balance, requires focus and patience. Wholeness must be first located inside ourselves in order to then manifest it in our external life.

and effectively and have a deep intuitive knowledge of how to do this. We may not think that we know how to heal, or even have any idea of how to go about it until we start, but if our intention is to heal and we allow our naturally wise and intuitive spirit self to take over, then the healing energy will flow and healing will occur.

The capacity for healing then, both for self-healing and for healing others, is a fundamental and inevitably present part of the human spirit. Certainly some of those among us are more naturally inclined to express themselves through a vocation in healing, and indeed may have extraordinary talents and abilities. However, as with music, we can also learn skills and tools, techniques and modalities, for focusing, channelling and refining our natural healing abilities for the good of others and ourselves.

Approaching life with a healing attitude

One of the greatest spiritual truths is that whatever we focus our attention upon, we give power to and attract into our lives. In this way we can cultivate and encourage our inner healer by continually, but gently, developing attitudes of mind that make more space for healing and the healer to show up in our lives.

Many of us have learned to be effective in life by becoming problem-solvers. We approach any new situation asking the question, 'Now what's the problem here?' We address any problem or dilemma by looking for the pathology, the thing that's not working, that needs to be fixed or replaced or removed altogether.

While this is successful as a problem-solving method, it trains us to be constantly looking for pathology and dysfunction and, lo and behold, the spiritual truth holds good, and more and more pathology and dysfunction shows up in our lives for us to address. We attract it by looking for it.

All of the same situations can be equally effectively addressed by asking a different question: 'How can I heal this? What does this situation need to make it whole, to make it work properly, and to restore peace and balance to it?'

The final outcome of both approaches may be similar, but the process that we have engaged in and the quality of energy that we have channelled is quite different. In one approach we have acted as a fault-finding, trouble-shooting, diagnostician. In the other we have acted as peace-bringer, restorer of balance and a healer.

How this affects our experience of the world is profound. Try it and feel how very different your daily experience of the world becomes. To cultivate a healing attitude is to cultivate compassion and grace. The more we use dowsing in our lives, the more we strengthen our connection with our spirit, and are able to ease and facilitate the dialogue between the different levels of our being. Our outer life becomes increasingly congruent and integral with our inner life.

Meditating on health

As well as focusing our intellectual energies on healing, we can also nurture those same qualities at their source in spirit. A simple self-healing meditation is of immense benefit and value, not only for enhancing our own health but also for strengthening our own healing capacity which can then be used to help others.

The following meditation will greatly nurture your inner healer, changing the way that people relate to you, and how you relate to your life.

Sit quietly with a relaxed, erect spine. Pay attention to your breathing without trying to control it, and visualize yourself in a column of light.

Visualize and become aware of the flame of your spirit dancing in your heart. Imagine it there as a

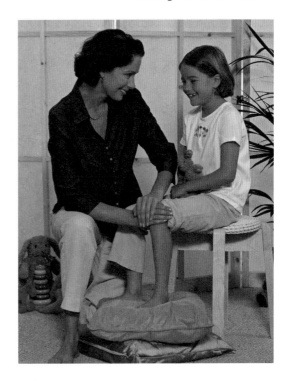

▲ While some have a deep sense of healing as a vocation, all of us have the inborn capacity to channel healing when the need arises.

bright flame like that of a candle, only much more vivid and intense, a fire burning in your heart and vitalizing the centre of your humanity.

Now let your attention move, scanning through your body, your emotions and your mind. Find any areas of tension, be they physical, emotional or mental. Using your imagination, take the tense, stored energy from those places, leaving them relaxed and full of ease, the energy flowing gently and harmoniously through them.

Take the blocked energy, and gently and lovingly place it into the fire. Watch as it burns and disappears, the energy is still present within you, but is now transformed. Ask that it be transformed into an energy of truth and beauty.

Continue placing any tense, dark, stuck, angry or fearful energy into the fire of your spirit, repeatedly asking that it be transformed into truth and beauty. When you are fully relaxed and at peace you are complete.

Dowsing the wheel of life

We live in a culture that relates to time as something linear. Primal cultures live much more intimately with their landscape, in harmony with the cycles of day, month, season and year, to inevitably return and begin anew that circular journey.

A belief in linearity and unending growth creates a dysfunctional relationship with our energetic environment. It causes us to deny the inevitable nature and fundamental health of the circle. At the most physical level, our current economies are built on the premise of indefinite growth, in progress and expansion. This is not a consciousness that helps the promotion of health.

The sacred circle

Many spiritual traditions represent spirit by a circle. It is a map of consciousness, showing how energy moves in time and space. The philosophy can be understood by following the cycle around

▲ The circle maps the movement of energy. Dowsing shows us where the pulse has reached, and the location and nature of any trauma.

▼ By observing the reflection of the outer cycles of nature on the inner cycles of our life – like that of the trees on the water – we perceive our own nature by the patterns we create.

the wheel of the year. In the north it is midwinter. This is the point of greatest contraction and introversion. We are most intimate with ourselves and each other. Now turn to the north-east. An imperceptible expansion is occurring. The ground begins to thaw and the seeds stir in the soil, unseen, and begin to grow.

We arrive in the east and the spring equinox. This is a time of visible expansion and growth, the shoots are above the ground and reaching for the sky. We come to the south-east, a time of flowering, pollination and fertility. Now we reach the south and midsummer. Plants are maturing, and the energy is transforming and gathering into seed heads. We come to the south-west and west, the harvesing first of grain and later of fruit.

At the beginning of autumn we reach the northwest. Now, the vegetation is dying back, and the energy is returning to the soil. Seeds are sown that will lie dormant until spring, gestating.

Everything in our lives inevitably follows a cycle. Some of these cycles are short, some are longer. We can look to see at what point on the circle our different projects or endeavours lie.

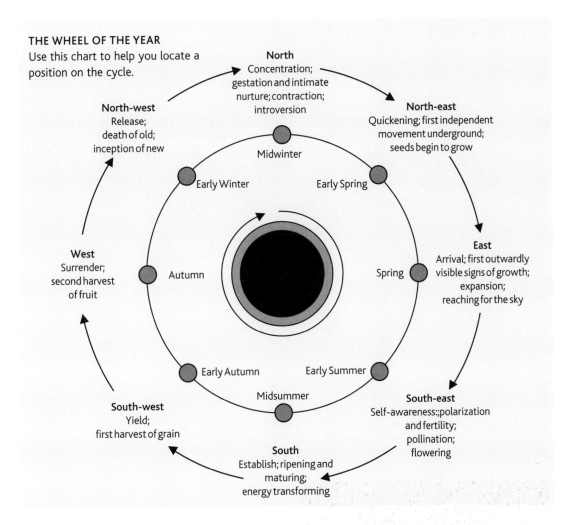

THE WHEEL OF THE YEAR
Use this chart to help you locate a position on the cycle.

North
Concentration; gestation and intimate nurture; contraction; introversion

North-west
Release; death of old; inception of new

North-east
Quickening; first independent movement underground; seeds begin to grow

Midwinter

Early Winter

Early Spring

West
Surrender; second harvest of fruit

Autumn

Spring

East
Arrival; first outwardly visible signs of growth; expansion; reaching for the sky

Early Autumn

Early Summer

South-west
Yield; first harvest of grain

Midsummer

South-east
Self-awareness; polarization and fertility; pollination; flowering

South
Establish; ripening and maturing; energy transforming

There are many profound images of health to be found in the circle. One important aspect is seeing how the degenerative, contractive phase is actually a healthy and necessary part of the cycle. It is a time of replenishment which will feed the generative side of the cycle. Death of the old must come before the birth of the new, liberating the energy required for re-investment and recreation.

For the cycle of life to continue, the energy must flow freely around it. Trauma, whether physical, emotional or mental, can be seen in this way, and healing can be understood in terms of easing and releasing the contracted and stuck energy, allowing it to then continue the cycle. This perspective gives us insight which can help to support healing.

Dowsing the circle

Consider a situation in your life where energy has stopped flowing, and where you feel stuck. You may or may not be conscious of the trauma that is responsible. Many traumas stem from childhood and are present as fears or misguided beliefs of personal inadequacy.

Dowsing in the usual way, you can ask where on the wheel of life the energy has become stuck. See if you can relate to the nature of the trauma and the energy block indicated.

Identifying energy flow in these terms can give powerful awareness for healing ourselves. Visualize the trauma dissolving, and energy starting to move freely around the circle once again.

The embrace of wholeness

Many of the things that we have explored in this book may seem new and unfamiliar and perhaps a little strange or challenging. We are not generally used to the thought that the answers to our questions and concerns of our life are available to us in the most simple way. We are more familiar with the expectation that guidance in our lives comes from outside of us, from people who seem to know more or appear to see further than us.

Of course, we can draw inspiration and learn enormously from everyone that we meet. Whether they are contemporary or historical figures they may be teachers and role-models for us in particular areas of our lives. However, each one of us is truly unique and the circumstances and details of our lives make it virtually impossible for anyone else to truly guide us along our life-path.

Incorporating the spirit

The ultimate guiding lights and points of reference for us are almost invariably spiritual ones. However, most of us spend the greatest amount of

▼ Meditation strengthens and deepens the connection between body, mind and spirit.

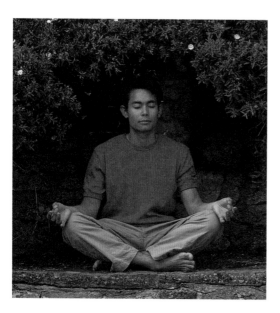

our energy focused on physical, mental and emotional concerns. How to incorporate the energy and relationship of spirit into our life can be a dilemma for us, an added burden that seems to be in contradiction to the many pressing material concerns that we have to meet. Perhaps the path that reconciles this dilemma is to integrate our sense of the spiritual into every part of our physical, emotional and mental activity.

Spirituality has become associated almost exclusively with religious practice. While it is indeed to be found there, it is not the only way of connecting with our spiritual selves.

Each of us is simultaneously a creature of body, mind and spirit. We are spiritually connected to everything that we think, feel and do. Seen in this light, the spiritual is not a separate part of our lives so much as an intimate, ever-present and interwoven reality. A glorious part of ourselves that can be re-activated and energized.

Opening to spirituality

Part of the reason that spirit remains unacknowledged is that we feel overwhelmed by something that we have no personal tools to deal with, or relate to. As with other matters, we have become accustomed to seeking spiritual guidance from outside ourselves, feeling unskilled or even forgetful of how to open the doorway.

Dowsing is a simple but invaluable tool for opening that doorway. It offers each one of us a direct and personal way to interact with, experience the presence of, and seek guidance from the spirit. More than this, it allows our own spirit to become a totally present and integrated part of even the most mundane parts of our lives, from gardening and baking to business and healing. It creates a richness, awareness and a great sense of contentment and purpose that people often only dream of. As we trust and integrate the wisdom from our spirit more and more, the channel of information and inspiration deepens and strengthens and in its own way, without our having to worry or coax it along.

▲ The more we use dowsing in our lives, the more we strengthen our connection with our spirit and the different levels of our inner and outer life.

Learning to trust

The more we recognize our sense of inner rightness, the more we might discover that we can dowse without tools. In fact, after a while, we can dowse without even focusing on or thinking about it at all. It then becomes hard to say where dowsing starts or stops. The wisdom of our spirit becomes ever-present in a seamless and integrated way, facilitating our every decision and action without our having to consider it as a distinct and separate activity.

This process is a gentle and gradual one, and evolves at its own speed, and we gradually find that we need to use tools such as the pendulum, L-rods and others less and less in our dowsing. The dowsing tools can perhaps be considered as keys to open the door. Once we have opened it often enough, we no longer find that we need to lock it afterwards, or indeed, even to close it at all. We become increasingly secure in a profound sense of inner-knowing or sense of rightness about things which the process of dowsing introduces us to and teaches us familiarity with.

To move towards this, you may like to experiment by visualizing a pendulum or L-rods in your mind's eye as you ask your dowsing question, and watch the response of your visualized tool. You may also scan an area with your hands and pay attention to changes in temperature or tingling sensations that you experience. Many dowsers use their whole body for deviceless dowsing, and experience a physical and mental relaxation, peace and ease at their 'Yes' response and a stiffening and tensing experience to indicate 'No'. These responses are all highly individual. Explore what works best for you.

With this unfolding of spiritual integration, the promise of original health will be fulfilled for you. You will find yourself naturally and intuitively choosing to do what your body needs to be healthy, choosing to engage with what your mind needs for stimulation and satisfaction, and finding yourself celebrating in the self-expression and fulfilment of your spirit's purpose.

Index

Useful addresses

Dr. Patrick MacManaway
108 West Street
Winooski
Vermont 05404
USA
+1.802.363.6783

Dr. Patrick MacManaway
West Bank Natural Health
Centre
Strathmiglo
Fife KY14 7QP
UK
+44.7707.639.293

www.patrickmacmanaway.com

British Society of Dowsers
+44 (0) 16845 576 969
www.britishdowsers.org
info@britishdowsers.org

American Society of Dowsers
+1 802 684 3417
www.dowsers.org
asd@dowsers.org

The Dowsers Society of New
South Wales
www.dowsingaustralia.com

The Canadian Society of
Dowsers
www.canadiandowsers.org

About the author

Dr. Patrick MacManaway is a dowser and holistic therapist. He trained first in dowsing and healing therapies with his parents, holistic pioneers Bruce and Patricia MacManaway, who established the Westbank Healing and Teaching Centre in Strathmiglo, Scotland in 1959. After completing a degree in medicine at the University of Edinburgh, he pursued his personal interest in holistic environmental studies by taking a two-year apprenticeship in Western geomancy and studying Feng Shui. Past-President of the British Society of Dowsers, he specializes in health problems and psychic disturbances in sick buildings and sad houses, and in enhancing health and productivity in domestic, commercial and agricultural spaces.He has an international consulting and teaching practice working regularly in the UK, USA and Australia, with offices at the Westbank Centre in Fife, Scotland and in Winooski, Vermont, USA. His great love is to spend time in nature and to explore, experience and enjoy health and holism.